WHAT LIES WITHIN
A Chronicle From Tragedy to Triumph

by
Gregory Allen Patterson

Order this book online at www.trafford.com/07-1489
or email orders@trafford.com

Most Trafford titles are also available at major online book retailers.

© Copyright 2008 Catherine Branch Patterson.

All rights reserved. No part of this publication may be reproduced, stored in a retrieval system, or transmitted, in any form or by any means, electronic, mechanical, photocopying, recording, or otherwise, without the written prior permission of the author.

Note for Librarians: A cataloguing record for this book is available from Library and Archives Canada at www.collectionscanada.ca/amicus/index-e.html

Printed in Victoria, BC, Canada.

ISBN: 978-1-4251-3753-3

We at Trafford believe that it is the responsibility of us all, as both individuals and corporations, to make choices that are environmentally and socially sound. You, in turn, are supporting this responsible conduct each time you purchase a Trafford book, or make use of our publishing services. To find out how you are helping, please visit www.trafford.com/responsiblepublishing.html

Our mission is to efficiently provide the world's finest, most comprehensive book publishing service, enabling every author to experience success. To find out how to publish your book, your way, and have it available worldwide, visit us online at www.trafford.com/10510

www.trafford.com

North America & international
toll-free: 1 888 232 4444 (USA & Canada)
phone: 250 383 6864 ♦ fax: 250 383 6804
email: info@trafford.com

The United Kingdom & Europe
phone: +44 (0)1865 722 113 ♦ local rate: 0845 230 9601
facsimile: +44 (0)1865 722 868 ♦ email: info.uk@trafford.com

10 9 8 7 6 5 4 3 2

Foreword

No one is exempt from challenges; but it is our reaction to challenges, and our commitment to press ahead and overcome them, that drastically impacts the outcome.

A songwriter once wrote, "I never knew love like this". Until I met Allen Patterson, I never knew love. I never knew faith. I never knew strength, courage, or passion, as I would come to know them through the beautiful and rewarding friendship God allowed me to share with Allen.

Completely unaware of the major life lessons God had in store for me, (and everyone else who has been blessed by Allen's presence); I made a conscious decision to introduce myself after hearing portions of his testimony at our church. Sinfully intrigued by his breathtaking smile, his luring voice, and pleasant spirit, yet disheartened by the tragedy that had so drastically distorted his life, I was fully convinced that me, my "Christian" goodness, and my perky personality was just what Allen needed for a brighter day and maybe even a better tomorrow.

Surprisingly, my intrusion into Allen Patterson's life failed to produce the pity party I had imagined he would host. Instead, I quickly came to know and love a man who was the true epitome of tragedy to triumph. I found myself in a place of witnessing, first hand, the truest and highest form of forgiveness, walking by faith, and victorious living, in spite of all circumstances. Instead of being the vessel of light for Allen that I had so adamantly set out to be, Allen became my light. He became my motivation to live life at its fullest, to "check" myself, and to dig deeply within my soul to see what is hidden that does not reflect God.

The powerful and life-changing lessons we learn from Allen Patterson and "What Lies Within" is to embrace and acknowledge every blessing, never to take life for granted, and to live with absolutely no regrets. His story clearly illustrates that life can be drastically and permanently altered in a moment.

Allen Patterson saw the world from two different perspectives as a result of this random victimization. The book inspires each of us to be less judgmental or condemning when we consider someone else's predicament.

Finally, the power of forgiveness is an essential part of healing, and Allen lived his life as an example of faith and forgiveness intertwined. He was a living testament to the strengthening, healing, and restoring power of God's love and forgiveness.

Thank you Allen for showing us the way. Your impact on the lives of others has been immeasurable, and your life and legacy will not be forgotten.

Tamara McLaughlin Patterson

WHAT LIES WITHIN
A Chronicle From Tragedy to Triumph

Table of Contents

Chapter 1: Introduction 4

Chapter 2: 10/13/95 10

Chapter 3: The Hospital 24

Chapter 4: New Jersey — What's Next? 52

Chapter 5: Journey Home: "Home, Sweet Home" 67

Chapter 6: What Now? – Reality Check 83

Chapter 7: Moving On 100

Chapter 8: Responding to Adversity –Why Not Me? 117

Chapter 9: As I Go On 130

Chapter 10: Going Home 134

CHAPTER 1: INTRODUCTION

What lies behind us and what lies before us are tiny matters to what lies within us. **-Oliver Wendell Holmes**

When I look back over my life, I see a life that has been filled with myriad experiences; ranging from total happiness and security to complete and utter despair. If someone was to illustrate my life thus far in storybook form, he may find it difficult to characterize that story. The dramatic highs and lows are simply overwhelming.

Would my life be characterized as a comedy or a tragedy; maybe it would fall somewhere in between? Certainly, it is an irony. One filled with twists and turns, ups and downs, joy and pain. When we read of personal stories and biographies of individuals who have overcome the perils and pitfalls of life to accomplish great things, it energizes us to persevere through tough times. And when we read of those stories wherein the main character has been overcome by tragic circumstances, particularly, early in life, it brings about a certain amount of empathy toward that tragic figure's plight. With that concern comes a degree of affiliation and identification with our personal battles that sometimes leaves us feeling sympathetic to those in less fortunate circumstances, and thus, and more grateful of our own good fortune.

Examples of such life experiences are in constant circulation throughout each of our media outlets, seemingly pleading some sort of emotional response from us all. This bombardment of tragedy and desperation that we are forced to hear and see on a daily basis can certainly leave behind a sour taste, and distort our outlook toward the life we lead and the world we live in. The tragic stories, over time, perpetuate for so long that we become somewhat indifferent toward them. After a while, stories of triumph no longer inspire and the tragic stories no longer educate; they just begin to sound like broken records repeating the same old song, again and again.

The truth is that we all have a story. We all have a story to tell… and somebody, somewhere needs to hear it. In fact, much of what we experience (good or bad) is designed specifically for us to share with a particular individual or group. I believe that our testimonies and stories, somehow take on lives of their own — just for the purposes of benefiting someone else, later on. The lessons that we learn from our experiences and trials are not necessarily there for our personal gain, but more so, they are to be shared with those following us who may be experiencing the same or similar difficulties. Thus, our respective lives serve as guideposts, directions, and inspiration for others to follow. So, when we selfishly withhold our experiences from others and keep them locked up inside of us, we are performing a disservice to many, and a disgrace to ourselves.

Because of this conviction that I have, I feel that it is of the utmost importance that I share my personal story. Maybe, it will be viewed as "just another sad song" and be buried among the bookshelves with countless numbers of testimonials, barely even noticed.Or, just maybe, there is one individual who is in a completely desperate situation and needs to read this manuscript! Maybe, it is tailor-made for that individual, crafted specifically for his/her circumstance! Maybe the publication of this book will help define and fulfill my true purpose in life.

Most of my early memories in life are very pleasant... somewhat. I can't claim that I was raised in some horrific environment and survived dire and challenging circumstances. In fact, my early childhood years were filled with many wonderful moments and accomplishments. For as long as I can recall I had always succeeded at everything. I always excelled in school, sports, and any popularity contests, as well. I grew up as a well-liked youth with a multitude of friends and family around me who always showered a tremendous amount of care and support, as I came along. I did, however, grow up in a single-parent household for most of my life. But, even though I grew up as a kid of divorce, I was still fortunate enough to have the support and DISCIPLINE from both parents. Therefore, I am unable to introduce my life, as one that began with challenges all around; one that was marked for destruction or devastation. Indeed, my life began like many others and was relatively unassuming in nature.

Many heroic individuals we read about are born into lives of despair, and they somehow manage to persevere by scratching and clawing through obstacles and challenges, and breaking through barriers like: racism, sexism, poverty, etc., in order to achieve great things. These are the kind of stories that I love to hear about and they are stories that are overwhelmingly inspirational. Alas, I am unable to stake claim to this kind of upbringing. The setting for the stage that would become my life was quite different and unexpected.

To be certain, I did not grow up in a home surrounded by a white picket fence, with bright red shutters, and 2.5 pets to match. In reality, my family faced its fair share of troubles. Being born to an interracial couple in the mid-seventies, even in rural North Carolina, shouldn't seem too unusual. But, my mother still recounts stories of when my father and she faced much adversity just because of their race. Even with a newborn baby boy, they found it difficult to find jobs, lodging, or even acceptance of any sort, because of their interracial marriage. In fact, for the first three months of my life, they had to settle in a literal shack located in the rear of someone else's property. Nonetheless, they persevered and managed to provide a safe and warm home for my younger brother and me, as we grew up.

By today's standards, my upbringing was very much typical in today's society and probably provides very little "excitement" for a manuscript about one's life. However, because of it I did grow into a fairly well adjusted young man. My teenage years represented a stage of growth where I really begin to develop a certain character that would prepare me for the things that lay ahead.

Early on, I began to develop a tremendous amount of self-confidence and determination, believing that I could achieve anything that I set out to accomplish. Even though it sounds much like a common attitude of many young people, it is not always a given that young people today truly recognize their potential. And little did I know at that time, but I would need that same kind of attitude in order to survive the critical events that were just ahead.

Without question, my attitude and self-awareness was really aided by the environment in which I was raised, as well as, the multitudes of accolades and achievements I received as a teen. My brother and I had walls of certificates and trophies as rewards for our achievements, both academically and athletically. The recognition certainly fueled and fed the belief that I had in myself, at the time. To me, the sky was indeed, the limit.

Though I realized tremendous success in my life at a very early age, my character wasn't by any means, flawless. As the accolades continued to pour in throughout my high school years, so would the exalted perception I had of myself. Additionally, I had no difficulty adapting socially and was well-liked among my peers and most others that I came in contact with. But with an increasing self-esteem also came an increasing interest in self-destructive behaviors.

Being a well-liked young man who often became the "life of the party" in many instances, turned out to have serious consequences. I quickly began to delve into overindulgence in the "party life," a mistake that many young people make. And I slowly began to lose focus on my academic goals and lose hold to a previously firm grip on inevitable success. I began to overindulge in many negative habits that oftentimes accompany that sort of lifestyle like: promiscuity and alcohol and drug abuse. This battle persisted throughout high school and into my college years at the state university where I was accepted.

After beginning my college career, I seem to have been reinvigorated, probably, by the general atmosphere and tenor of accomplishment that is present on many campuses. Being surrounded by so much potential and opportunity helped reenergize my focus on achieving a successful and productive life. And even though the personal battles persisted, my optimistic outlook on life returned, now stronger than ever! At this point, I developed a "map" of my future life. In other words, I was creating a step-by-step plan of what course my life would take and exactly how it would wind up. My plan for myself was direct and definitive, in my mind. First, I would successfully obtain my degree (with honors, no doubt!) Then, I would generate a successful entrepreneurial endeavor that would generate millions for my future family and me. Sound familiar? Sure it does. It sounds like the rallying call and battle cry for many young, motivated men and women, everywhere; many of whom are sadly disillusioned. Indeed, it was a worthwhile goal and ideal plan to have. But I submit this question, as will my entire story; what do you do when your best laid plans become the worst-case scenario?

At age 19, in the midst of my best and brightest days, I would face the darkest, most unimaginable predicament. Almost instantaneously—and certainly unexpectedly—my life was completely interrupted. That most tragic turn of events threatened my outlook on life and my ability to live it. In the very crux of my young life, I would be caught completely unaware and virtually struck down. I would be forced into a position where my whole foundation would be tested beyond belief. This situation would test me on every side and make me examine who I was at the time—and who I would become. Every ounce of strength, optimism, belief, or hope that I possessed at the time would be put to the test. On the night of 10/13/1995, I would begin to discover what truly was within me.

CHAPTER 2: 10/13/95

Some days live on forever in infamy; the bombing Pearl Harbor; the assassinations of President Kennedy and Dr. Martin Luther King, Jr., and the day my life changed forever. Sure, to the rest of the world, it was just another day. But for me, the 13th of October 1995 was an omen of evil and enduring wickedness. That date will forever be etched in my heart and mind.

It was approximately 10 o'clock that Friday evening when me and two of my college buddies were riding down a Washington D.C. highway in route to my friend's parents' home, where we were visiting that weekend. Oh, the joy of being young and free. It had been a wonderful vacation thus far—a much-needed escape from the rigors of our studies. In retrospect, a quiet beach in the Caribbean may have been a better idea. However, the partying, nightlife, and social scene of D.C. were calling us, and we were ready to answer. We were welcomed by the most hospitable, friendliest family you can imagine. And since our arrival in Maryland, we had been catered to in every way by the Smith family. For three broke college students, this was certainly new and unusual; but very much appreciated. For all intents and purposes, things appeared to be a normal, but exciting, weekend for us. That would quickly change. And in a flash, that night would prove to be the most horrible, memorable, and life-changing night of our lives.

What started as a brisk Friday morning transitioned into a beautiful fall afternoon. The weather was perfect that day; comfortably warm and not a cloud in sight… just perfect for a road trip. Our day began around 8:00 a.m. after a long night of club-hopping. The excitement level was high as my roommate and I spotted our close friend and transportation for our upcoming weekend excursion. Our much-needed vacation had come in the form of a short road trip to Maryland, with the boys. We set out around 11:00 that morning on what seemed to be a typical day. The ride itself was uneventful as we darted in and out of traffic to arrive at our destination in record time.

Riverdale, Maryland, a Washington D.C. suburb, was our destination and home of my friend's relatives. It was really my first trip to that part of the country, and I was impressed by the comfortable surroundings of the town and more so, the home off our hosts. This was my first meeting with my friend's family, the Smiths. They were wonderful people who welcomed my roommate and me, as if we were part of the family. Tired and hungry from our road trip, we placed our bags in our temporary bedrooms for the weekend and sat down to eat the tantalizing homemade meal that was waiting for us.

After devouring this wonderful meal, which I still remember several years later, we sat down to watch the evening news—doing our best to catch up on the latest happenings while we faded in and out of slumber. Our bellies were full of fried chicken, so we tried hard not to "eat and sleep" off most of our mini vacation. Although it was hard to stay awake and pay attention to the mostly unfamiliar news, one story captured our full attention. The television news anchors began to discuss an event that was to be held a few days later and the publicity surrounding that event. The Million Man March was the event being spoken about, and the one story that sparked our interest. There had been a tremendous amount of buzz surrounding this event at our campus back in North Carolina. Personally, I had not heard much about the march until a few weeks previous. In Raleigh, many of the students were organizing bus trips to attend this huge event; as the anchor continued to talk, our interest grew. I believe that it was at that point during the newscasts that the three of us made our decision to attend the March three days later.

Interestingly enough, neither of us had any overwhelmingly strong political beliefs, but we all did believe that the advertised purpose—to protest violent behaviors and self-destructive attitudes that were rampant in the lives of young minority men—was certainly a worthwhile cause. Since we were supportive of that principle goal, we felt that it would be hypocritical for us not to attend. So we solidified our plans and included the Million Man March in our vacation itinerary.

The newscast moved on to other local events and sports, and we drifted off to sleep to rest up for our anticipated night of clubbing. Once again, we were planning to paint the town red, white, and blue—and take in the local nightlife. Earlier that day, we had been informed of a big concert that was to take place Friday night. Being the avid party goer that I was, I was thrilled at this opportunity to "live it up" at a new and different locale each night. Every detail of that night and the following days is still just as vivid as it was so many years ago. It's almost as if I relive the events over and over again. Sometimes it seems like hardly a day has passed.

The three of us jumped in the car around 8:00 p.m. intending to attack the D.C. nightlife. In addition to the party we were planning to attend, we had heard reports of several other events taking place that night in the surrounding areas.

We felt the proverbial "buzz in the air" as we panned the streets from our SUV searching for a place to go. After much deliberation, we then decided on a party destination; a concert on the grounds of the Robert F. Kennedy Memorial Stadium — better known as RFK Stadium — in the southern area of the city. So off to the party we went! We finally arrived there after about an hour of unintentional sightseeing. And like most men, we didn't stop to ask for directions. The destination was unfamiliar territory for all of us. After arriving there, we still sat in the SUV debating long and hard whether or not to relinquish the scarce funds we had to attend this party that seemed somewhat lackluster from the outside looking in. But as young and foolish minds do, we agreed that we had traveled too far not to carry on. So we did.

Our decision was made, so we paid our ten bucks to go in. Immediately after entering the building I felt extremely uncomfortable and totally out of place. Maybe it was because everyone in line was being frisked thoroughly; generally a bad sign. Now don't misunderstand, I have been to plenty of concerts and parties, but in this instance I thought to myself, "I have never seen security like this. I wonder what else is going on." Everyone in the line was forced to remove their shoes and hand them over to security. Airport security has nothing on these guys. I know that a light should have gone off in my head, but it didn't. If security is this tight, then just maybe I shouldn't be in here. Or, maybe that light did go off but I just ignored it. Like so many young people do, I made the tragic mistake of ignoring that still small voice inside of me that's usually trying to keep you safe — and out of trouble. I've come to believe that the "still small voice" is the voice of reason that God places in all of us, that tells us when something is wrong or when we are about to participate in something that is potentially harmful for us.

Nonetheless, I continued forward into the concert Hall. Up until then, the entire day had been packed with excitement, but now a feeling of total discomfort began to overwhelm us. This, supposedly festive event, suddenly began to feel like a mistake. But we shook off the feeling and tried our best to enjoy ourselves that night and repress the discomfort that we all shared.

In the beginning, we just wanted to stand far away from the crowds of people pouring in, and just enjoy the music. However, our attempts to put ourselves at ease by creating distance between us and the rest of the crowd proved to be ineffective as the crowd grew larger and larger. I, myself, felt very much like a "fish out of water." There I was, an avid party goer, who couldn't enjoy himself in a huge concert like this! As time went on, the three of us began to loosen up a little. We soon joined the majority and began to dance. We danced for a while without any disturbances in the arena. Then, the atmosphere began to clear as the audience eased into their party mode. Just moments ago, the tension in the air was stifling. And now everyone seemed to be in a relaxed, jovial mood.

Consequently, we let down our guard, ignored our gut instincts and continued to party with the rest of the crowd. I'm sure it's true that hindsight has 20/20 vision. After much reflection on this experience, and years of observation of current states of affairs regarding the barometer of our country's inner cities, it is disturbing that so many young people have to live their lives constantly looking over their shoulders. Now, I don't necessarily condone this "party all the time" mindset that infuses the minds of many of our young people, including myself, at the time. But, it is a reality that exists and always has, for that matter. The disturbing thing is that young people are constantly in fear of being caught in the middle of crossfire, as if they were in a battle zone. And something about that night made us feel like we had stepped into enemy territory.

As expected, there was the usual drama that accompanies the party scene. There were several disturbances in the arena which prompted the bands to "close-up shop." The organizers turned on the lights as the people began to pour out of the gym. We were one of the first groups to exit the chaos. As we approached the vehicle, my buddy, Chris hopped into the passenger seat of the car, and I, into the back of the car. Soon after that, for some odd reason, the two of us exchanged seats. At the time, what seemed to be an awfully meaningless and minor event would later prove to be major and life-altering.

The three of us exited the grounds on which the concert was taking place and headed toward the interstate, homeward bound. As we were weaving through the streets of the surrounding neighborhood, there was a strong sense of relief in the atmosphere. I was extremely relieved to be safely away from the concert grounds. The overwhelming discomfort and uneasiness that had encompassed my body earlier finally began to wear off for the first time since we left home early that evening. Me and my buddies began to deliberate over a brief sightseeing tour of some of Washington D.C.'s more desirable attractions, before calling it a night.

This was the first time I had spent any considerable time in the city, and I wanted to visit Howard University and a few other landmarks. After a short time, we all agreed that was the best choice.

The very next thing I remember was passing a car identical to the car we were in. As a matter of fact, as we passed this car, I commented to the others just how similar this black SUV was. That bit of trivia seemed insignificant at the time, so we paid little attention to it. But now, looking back, I am amazed at how every single detail of that evening is so vividly clear in my memory. I never knew how much those details or those memories would mean: the trees, the weather, our clothing, everything. Everything about our surroundings that evening is still clearly visible in my mind.

We continued on, virtually ignoring this vehicle and every other vehicle we passed, in route to the interstate. In just a few minutes, we entered onto the DC Beltway, heading northbound toward home. We began speeding down this dark, empty highway. I remember staring out the window and admiring the view of RFK Stadium from there (I am a huge football fan!). My friend and I began a deep conversation while my roommate laid down in the back seat for a quick nap. I don't remember what we were talking about; but, whatever it was, it must have been heavy. As we were deeply involved in this discussion and enjoying the tune playing on the radio in the background, we noticed a car entering onto the highway in front of us. As we casually passed to the left of this vehicle—a light metallic colored sedan—it was noticeably slowing down as they continued to travel. We eased around this car that seemed to be the only other vehicle in sight. As we drove by, I caught a brief glimpse of the individuals inside. It was only a split second, but, the image I remember was an awfully unpleasant one. There were three young men in the car, with their eyes fixed on us in a cold, stone-faced stare. All kinds of alarms went off in my head, but I continued my discussions with the driver and gave little thought to the strangers in the car we had just passed. But, the next few moments created an awfully unpleasant feeling down in my gut.

Shortly, I began to replay this brief encounter in my mind, as if some force was pulling at my conscience, not allowing me to overlook this seemingly insignificant encounter. In retrospect, this felt like a voice telling me, better yet, warning me to beware of those individuals we had just passed on the highway. I still remember checking the rearview mirror a few times before silencing that voice, and dismissing it as my own delusions and paranoia. I even recall purposely lowering my head and leaning forward as to tie my shoes. Then, my next thought was that, 'this is absolutely ridiculous; why am I ducking?' 'What am I afraid of?' I even began to laugh at myself as I resumed the conversation with my friend.

I don't know exactly how much time had passed since we passed the carpool of strangers; maybe only two or three minutes, however, so many thoughts and fears, suddenly overwhelmed my mind. But why? At that moment, everything seemed fine. My roommate was asleep in the back seat, and the two of us were enjoying ourselves in the front.

For whatever reason, I couldn't shake the feeling that I had. One brief observation of other passengers on the road created an overwhelming sense of uneasiness and fear in me. Suddenly, just as I began to dismiss this ridiculousness for what it was, the worst and most unimaginable thing occurred.

I was looking straight ahead when something struck me with the force of a wrecking ball.

A bullet, fired from that vehicle, pierced the car door and crashed into my neck. My arms flew up into the air from the tremendous force of the impact. The impact from the gunshot generated an excruciating pain as though the bullet had shattered my spine. I was immediately rendered helpless and fell over into the middle of the front seats only to be supported by a seatbelt strapped across my chest.

The entire scene appeared to be in slow motion. I remember hanging over the seatbelt, looking out of the window, and seeing the fire from the continuous gun blasts coming from the rear window of this passing vehicle. There was no sound, however; just a slow-motion panorama of this chaotic scene being played out before my eyes. The most horrifying aspect was seeing my own blood profusely shooting out of the side of my neck. I had been shot!

It was an overwhelming shock, to say the least. There was fear… tremendous fear and the instant realization that my whole life had just changed, instantaneously. My whole reality had changed from a completely carefree 19-year-old, just minutes before, to someone in a helpless state of survival — struggling to catch my next breath.

My Prayer:
In the midst of the chaos which surrounded me, my world at the time was a completely soundless one. Even though, I could see that sparks of gunfire coming from the vehicle beside us, and there were frantic screams for help by my fellow passengers, I couldn't hear a thing. I attempted to cry for help while looking up at the driver, but there was no response; or so it seemed. Thinking back, maybe he was trying to dodge gunfire at the time. I even tried to bark out

instructions on the best way to get me out of there, but there was nothing. I couldn't talk at all, and the only thing I could move was my bottom lip. This is when I realized just how critical my situation was. At this point I knew that I was completely helpless, and I didn't know what to do about it.

    The shooting, which seemed like it would never stop, eventually did. The attack, which probably lasted less than one minute, was a relentless assault for which there seemed to be no possible escape. My guess is that they finally ran out of bullets. I was told later, by the driver, that he attempted to reverse the car to escape the assault only to see the attackers reverse their car and continue shooting. They actually continued to chase us, in reverse, on the interstate. That is, until another vehicle that was traveling in the correct direction almost crashed into them, causing them to speed off. Just the image of this scene occurring in the middle of a major highway is mind-boggling to me. The mere possibility of something like that happening is difficult to fathom. Who knows… maybe I should be thanking that person for their part in saving my life.

    Life can change in an instant. Just as the smoke cleared, everyone's energy began to shift from taking cover to attempting to keep me alive.

    I lay there, attempting to communicate with my friends, and I began to hear and understand the words of encouragement as well as the fear, panic, and desperation, coming from their mouths. The driver sped off, frantically trying to find the nearest hospital. At this time, I literally felt the life slowly escaping from my body. I was losing severe amounts of blood and quickly losing consciousness. I can remember seeing streams of blood squirting from my neck. I could no longer breathe, and I started to frantically gasp for air. I remember encouraging myself with all that I had, to just, stay awake. (I don't believe I have ever felt a stronger urge to fall asleep, in my life!) I could hear the car speeding down the highway, along with my friends' urgings to stay awake and hang in there with them. I felt somewhat optimistic that I would be OK, if I could only, *stay awake*.

In spite of their best attempts to encourage me, I began to "slip away" faster and faster. In my mind, I had already begun to accept the reality that this was probably the end for me as my personal resolve drastically weakened with unconsciousness and imminent death drawing closer and closer. At that very moment, hopelessness had set into my consciousness and I began to reflect on my family and ponder their well-being without me around any more.

"Here I am at 19 years old; murdered in a vehicle on a dark, lonely highway," I thought to myself. However, something inside of me wouldn't allow me to feel sorry for myself for too long. "I have lived a full, fortunate life until now," I reasoned. Surprisingly enough, for someone as young as I was—who had been 'gunned down in the street' for no apparent reason, I was able to find comfort in my heart with what was happening. My seemingly apparent death no longer frightened me as I contemplated my next and most crucial steps in this frightening course of events.

My friends were racing down the highway at a frantic pace in an attempt to get me to a hospital. With the hospital miles away from us (we later calculated that the hospital was at least a 20-minute drive away), I still can only imagine what they must have felt as they watched me lying there bleeding profusely and slowly losing consciousness. I'm sure from their perspective, the feelings of despair and fear must have been overwhelming. One of their closest friends was dying in front of them. By this time, I was no longer concerned with arriving at the hospital. Deep down I felt that what I really needed was far more in-depth than anything a hospital could offer. Yes, I needed medical attention. Yes, my body was breaking down. Yes, life-saving equipment was minutes away. But at times like that, you realize that it's not just your life that needs saving. My focus immediately shifted, and I began to find a refuge in prayer.

All of my life I had been surrounded by believers in God—in Jesus—and the Christian lifestyle had never really been too far from me. Though I spent most of my teenage years in rejection rather than acceptance of the reality of God, I never questioned the importance of our eventual acceptance of Him into our lives. Up until now, faith was something that could wait. I had too much living and partying to do without God cramping my style. I couldn't even use ignorance as an excuse. The only excuse I had—was that I had time. Now, I realized that my time had run out. This was my last chance, so I prayed.

My prayer to God was not for him to step in and rescue me from this awful situation; but, my prayer was for a different type of salvation. I began to pray the "sinner's prayer." In my wildest dreams, I never imagined that I would face such a severe call to change; (especially not at such a young age) but, this was the moment of truth. I prayed for Jesus Christ to come into my heart; into my life and become my personal savior. I asked Him to become the Lord of my life. This was an act that I had passed on countless times before in my young life. I guess that's why I was able to find comfort with what I thought was the end of my life. Maybe I felt partly responsible for what had happened to me, because I made the decision not to accept Him—as strange as that may sound. By no means am I suggesting that God caused this horrible thing to happen to me, but I often wonder if I had taken a different course in my lifestyle, whether or not I could have avoided this situation, altogether.

After praying to God, I immediately realized that every bit of resistance that I had in me had gone away. There wasn't any more fight left! I could no longer breathe, nor could I see or hear anything that was going on around me. However, at that moment, just before losing consciousness, there was nothing but peace around and within me. The fear and confusion that had understandably encompassed me from the moment I was shot had gone, and for the first time in my young life my soul was completely at peace. Though I had come face to face with certain death, as I believed at that moment; I was comforted rather than discouraged. I was comforted by the fact that God heard my prayer and confident that, if this was the end of my natural life, I would spend eternity with Him.

Psalm 27:14 "Wait on the LORD: be of good courage, and he shall strengthen thine heart: wait, I say, on the LORD."

This was the first time in my life that I could actually feel His presence. It was nothing tangible that I could see or touch. But, I knew, without any doubt, that God was present. He was there, in that car with me. Sure, I had previous doubts about who He was. Much like many other human beings, I too had moments where I was confused about what I thought was God's apparent willingness to remain distant from us. Not that I ever questioned His existence, but, at times, I questioned His methods.

CHAPTER 3: The Hospital

A badly wounded vehicle carrying a badly wounded body finally arrived at Prince George's Hospital several miles away from the location where the shooting originally took place. More than 20 minutes had passed since the attack, and I was completely unconscious by the time we arrived at the hospital. So most of the story about what took place is based upon what my fellow passengers said, in addition to the reports from the medical staff.

The car pulled into the emergency room parking lot, full of bullet holes from the attack (The firefighter who later examined the vehicle counted at least 11 bullet holes, from what I was told). Bullets had pierced the car all throughout its body. Windows had been shattered, the gas line was hit and leaking fuel, and a couple tires had been hit but not yet gone flat. The very fact that the vehicle made it that far was indeed miraculous. As soon as we came to a stop in front of the emergency room, the vehicle's engine died. It was either from extreme fuel loss or the damage to the vehicle itself, but the car managed to get us to the hospital and out of harm's way — somewhat. It was as if some unseen force held that car together and steered it to the hospital, just in the nick of time.

In fact, we learned that the firemen and other emergency personnel were totally perplexed that the car made it that far based on a more thorough examination. "It was a miracle," they claimed, "that this car didn't explode on the highway!"

I was completely incapacitated when we arrived at the emergency room entrance. My friends frantically screamed for help from anyone in the area to assist them in getting me out of the car. From what I understand, there were several people in the area, but no one would help. Apparently, there were hospital staff close by, but they were somehow restricted from leaving the hospital doors to offer any assistance (which makes little sense to me). I was awfully surprised to hear about this sort of restriction, when clearly I was someone who needed help.

My friends had to carry me into the emergency room themselves. I can only imagine how difficult that must have been for them to carry my limp body, while trying to stabilize my head and neck, over a considerable distance from the vehicle to a table inside. My skin tone had turned completely blue from the lack of oxygen. No one knows exactly how long I went without oxygen, but it was a considerable amount of time. This was crucial information, because severe brain damage can occur shortly after that sort of suffocation takes place. Then, if there is no immediate CPR given to the victim, he may face certain death. At that point, I was practically face-to-face with death.

My friends managed to carry me to a table, and by that point, my condition had gone from critical to grave. I had long ago stopped breathing, and now my heart had completely stopped beating. At some point during the trip to the hospital, I slipped into cardiac standstill—basically a preceptor for flat-lining.

I'm told that the emergency personnel were somewhat hesitant to attend to me because they believed that it was too late to save me and there was little else that could be done. Granted, I can only share my friends' version of the events that took place, but from their perspective, the slightest hesitation or precautions taken would have been too long.

Apparently, the emergency room crew needed a little persuasion from my friends before they took any action. I thank God for this type of determination in friends. It is certainly rare, and it is what helped save my life.

The idea of any type of emergency personnel intentionally hesitating to administer medical assistance to anyone who's life is in danger, is horrifying, to say the least. I choose to think that for the most part, the majority of health care professionals put their heart and soul into their work. Unfortunately, there are too many cases where the high volume of trauma patients and relative lack of adequate staffing in many hospital settings contributes to negligent patient care.

The constant repetition of severe injury and death that hospital workers see day-in and day-out can surely damage one's psyche. When faced with these unfortunate realities, the most optimistic of caregivers could become slightly callous. It would be nearly impossible for someone working in that environment not to become that way.

In D.C., as with other major metropolitan areas, the number of similar incidents of violent crimes is astronomical. In an area where this type of scenario is commonplace, I imagine that it is easy for people to generalize these accidents and categorize all of the victims as willing participants in some sort of self-destructive lifestyle.

Tragically, the first reaction by many of the emergency personnel, when an attack occurs in one of these neighborhoods is, "they must have had it coming." But I didn't "have it coming." I was a college student. I was a good kid who basically stayed out of trouble. I came from a good home, and I had a great future ahead of me. I was on my way to the Million Man March. I didn't deserve this; nobody does. It's important that we not allow this form of familiarity to create contempt. I mean, we all should have the same chance at survival regardless of our backgrounds.

I am absolutely grateful to the hospital staff and feel fortunate to have gotten the treatment I received. Under divine providence, through the hands of those doctors, I was saved.

My experiences and observations since then have shown me that too often, cases like mine are generalized. I was—and continue to be—disappointed in the reporting of the incident by a lot of the media organizations that covered the story. I was informed of several newspaper and television reports that depicted us as some type of "thugs" who provoked the shootings. Such generalizations are a disservice to people who are victimized in similar ways; especially to those who lose their lives and receive this characterization, leaving nothing but tainted memories in their wake.

I can't help but wonder if this was the reason that the care I received wasn't very prompt, from my friends' viewpoint. Also, this has caused me to wonder about those shooting victims who may have contributed to their condition. Are they treated fairly, and do they receive the same medical attention and care as anyone else?

Nevertheless, after some deliberation over whether or not it would be even possible for them to save me, along with some helpful insistence by my companions, they proceeded with CPR procedures. All medical logic suggests that I should have suffered severe brain damage, at the very least. To an onlooker, I am sure that this graphic image must have looked similar to some tragic scene from the television show *ER*, with doctors and nurses scrambling to revive an almost lifeless body. The frantic shouts of medical jargon and constant stream of beeps in the background signify that the patient is nearing the end. It must have been a discouraging sight to see. I guess it's understandable to me why they were not very optimistic about my survival. Thank God they didn't give up on me!

The emergency room team performed a couple of other emergency procedures in order to "pull me out." They performed a tracheotomy procedure on my neck so that a respirator could be attached in order to generate manual airflow through my windpipe. At the same time, a heart defibrillator, a device designed to deliver a series of electric shocks to the heart, was applied to my chest to cause my heart to resume beating on its own. Both proved to be effective, and slowly but surely, I was revived. My heart started to pump again and my natural skin tone started to return as the respirator began to pump oxygenated air into my distressed lungs. After a prolonged struggle, life began to fill my body again.

Next, the medical staff needed to address the problem of the massive amounts of blood loss that occurred as a result of the shooting. To do so, they had to begin giving me a series of blood transfusions. Life has a predictable way of panning out. It is somewhat ironic that shortly before this shooting incident, I had voluntarily given blood at our campus "blood drive." And now, I was a needy recipient. Reflecting on this course of events shed a new light on the importance of donating blood. I suppose it's one of those things we don't fully grasp until we experience the need firsthand—or know someone who has.

The medical personnel had successfully revived me, and now I was breathing again with the help of a respirator. My condition, though very critical, slowly began to stabilize. As I eased back into consciousness, I'm sure there was a tremendous sense of relief among the medical staff, who worked so hard to save my life. I soon awoke to see a crowd of individuals surrounding me, there in the emergency room. Shortly after that, I experienced the full gamut of emotions as I began to realize exactly what had happened to me.

I can remember opening my eyes for the first time and exactly what my first thoughts were. The staff around me seemed to scurry into my eyesight once they realized that I had regained consciousness. There was a tremendous amount of relief and surprise inside of me. I was completely aware of my surroundings, and the memory of what took place earlier that night was still fresh. However, my last recollection of emotions was acknowledgment that my life was over. So, I was completely shocked to find myself alive and awake. I attempted to instruct them to relay a message to my family at home. I wanted to inform my family about what happened, and that I was OK. I don't think it was effective, being that, I couldn't talk at all. Nevertheless, I tried.

The next thing I remember was some guy—I assume he was a doctor from the way he was dressed—approaching my bedside. He proceeded to inform me of the severity of my injuries and some of the steps they took in order to assist me. Certainly, this is common dialog among emergency physicians and their patients. Doctors have a responsibility to fully disclose to patients and their families relevant medical issues and concerns, and any diagnosis of their conditions and the related prognosis for the future. This is particularly important for patients who have suffered critical injuries or sickness, and may not know the severity of their conditions. However, it was the delivery of his explanation to me that was rather disturbing. Bedside manner is of utmost importance during stressing moments such as this one, and I'm certain that most medical professionals handle the delivery of tragic news with extreme care. But what still haunts me to this day is not the information he gave to me, but the manner in which he gave it.

In his attempt to be forthright and realistic, this physician single-handedly discomforted and destroyed any remaining optimism that I did have, after waking up. He stared at me and in a smug fashion, proceeded to tell me that I had been paralyzed from the shooting. Furthermore, he stated that I would "never walk again." And just before abruptly walking away, he smirked and said to me, "look at what your 'brothers' have done to you. To this day, I don't know exactly what he meant by that statement.

My heart seemingly dropped down into my stomach upon hearing this news. Again, I was completely coherent at the time and was completely aware of my surroundings and circumstances. Furthermore, my mindset before this interaction with the doctor was absolutely peaceful and optimistic. I was overjoyed and amazed at the fact that I had survived. The peace of God and the joy of the Lord had filled my body. But this one encounter completely robbed me of any positive emotions that were inside of me. In a matter of seconds, this person (although, I'm sure it was unintentional) delivered an overwhelmingly destructive message to me at the most critical moment of my treatment—and had no consideration of the impact his words would carry. Yes, I needed to know the facts concerning my condition but, his timing and his delivery were completely inappropriate. I wonder how he would feel if he had to "walk a mile in my shoes."

Now, I have no intention of damaging anyone's character or placing accusations upon an individual's professionalism. But, after much reflection on this course of events, such examples of poor bedside etiquette continually reverberate in my mind, with thoughts of the resulting damage it may create. I can't help but to wonder whether I had been discriminated against because of how I had been injured. Maybe I was looked at as someone who somehow, some way, contributed to this unfortunate incident; or maybe I wasn't an innocent victim, but "I had it coming."

I seriously doubt that this was an attempt to discourage me. It was probably an example of bottled frustration resulting from his witness of countless numbers of senseless violent attacks, reaching a boiling point and pouring out at an inopportune time. Whether intentional or not, it had its effect, nonetheless. Its affect was completely spirit-breaking for me. I lay there for a moment, first unable to move, now, unable to dream. All hope had deserted me seemingly at the speed of light; just from a few words at a critical time.

This is certainly an example of the overwhelming power that words possess. The confessions we make, as well as those we allow to be made for us, greatly influence our outcome in a given situation. Before I was given the chance to exercise willpower in this battle for survival, my faith was shattered by someone's words. There, overwhelmed by confusion, fear, and discouragement, I didn't really care whether I lived or died anymore.

Maybe loneliness is the best way to describe the way I felt at that moment. It seemed like everyone had left the room and I was alone and stranded. As I lay there, staring at the ceiling, it felt as if everyone and everything; God, and even, hope, had deserted me. I was devastated, and my optimism was destroyed. What could I possibly do next?

Previously, after regaining consciousness, I thought "I am alive," and "all is well!" Now, all I could do was hopelessly stare at the ceiling. It was there, at my weakest, most disheartened moment, that I began to be comforted. Again, an overwhelming presence filled that room and I was suddenly encouraged. There weren't any bright lights or visions of tunnels, or anything like that; but, a calming force had encompassed me at a time when calmness should have been far from me, by all accounts. This, to me, felt much like a fog, surrounding my body and shielding me from the negativity throughout the hospital room.

Negativity, in the form of a bad report, pessimism, disappointment, etc., (ever-present in such environments), had successfully penetrated my mind in a flash. But, this presence which represented comfort, peace, and security; served as protection for me, in this most fragile state. That presence, undoubtedly, was God. The spirit of God was there with me, beside me, inside of me. When I had no reason to find comfort and confidence in my prognosis for the future, or even, for that night, He assured me that I had nothing to worry about.

I didn't hear any sounds, or audible voices. I could hear a "still, small voice" planted within me, telling me, "you are mine, and I'll take care of you." This, I immediately received as confirmation that I would survive. Not only that, this gave me the confidence that I would see many days thereafter, and that my health would be completely restored! This was a confidence that kept me in these early days following the shooting incident and has kept me since then. It's one that I will continue to stand on from now on.

Friday, October 13, 1995, was a day that I will never forget. The events which took place on that day are chiseled into my mind like a manuscript that is carved into stone tablets, destined to remain forevermore. A painful memory such as this will never be erased, not by time or circumstances. Each moment of that day, vividly appears in my mind as if it were yesterday. What began as a typical day would turn into the most unbelievable and most difficult, that I have ever seen—and probably will ever see, again.

My life was flipped upside down and completely rearranged in a matter of seconds. This is something that I, personally, could not conceive happening to me. I was very much aware of common tragedies that occur at the most unexpected times to the most unsuspecting people. However, I couldn't fathom anything like that, coming my way. Why would it? Trouble, was usually the last thing on my mind. But, on that day, trouble somehow found me.

Nevertheless, this was the hand that I was dealt, and so I have to play by the rules. This was my new reality. My life from this point on would never be the same. Not that I believed the report that I was given that night—the report that I would never walk again (if I survived the beginning days)—but yet, I have to accept the current circumstances as part of my fate. The challenges and obstacles that were ahead of me would be an unbelievable test of my will, and more importantly, my faith. Later, that night I was airlifted to a shock-trauma unit in Baltimore. The toughest times were in front of me, and unbeknownst to me, my struggle for survival had just begun.

BALTIMORE

I arrived at my destination, a shock-trauma ward, at the University of Maryland-Baltimore. I was completely unconscious and incapacitated during this flight. The helicopter which transported me from my previous hospital location swiftly arrived on the helipad above the hospital in time for me to receive the next phase of treatments. Initially, I was revived and then stabilized in the emergency room at PG County Hospital. At this point, I wasn't quite "out of the woods" yet, from a health standpoint. There was still a significant amount of treatments to be done in order for me to survive through the early days. Even though I was somewhat stable, my condition was still considered critical. PG County Hospital did not have the resources for an intense, long-term plan of care like the one I would need, so my journey began.

I would remain at this hospital in intensive care for nearly two months. This period of time was filled with the toughest phase of my journey through recovery, both physically and emotionally. The severity of my condition really began to become real to me and to those around me. But, it was the psychological battles I struggled with the most, and that nearly destroyed my resolve.

My first recollection of life in the Baltimore shock-trauma unit was waking up on a hospital bed being whisked through the hallways. I was en route to a room filled with what seemed to be space-age equipment; something similar to an equipment room on a TV space ship. Those humongous pieces of equipment were used to perform scans on my brain and spinal cord. The tests, a CT scan and MRI, were completely frightening to me. My psychological state had regressed tremendously since arriving in Baltimore. Needless to say, having my whole body placed on a "tray" and shoved inside this strange machine, into a deep, dark hole, was an unpleasant and terrifying experience. This is especially true if you have no clue as to what is going on and no ability to do anything about it.

After examining the extent of damage to my spinal cord and discovering that there was no physiological signs of brain damage (I don't believe there was any, although some of my friends might disagree), the physicians inserted a stint into an artery in my leg. This was weird, because I had to watch this procedure on a monitor that was in front of us. I didn't understand at the time, but this was an important procedure. It was designed to prevent any blood clots that might form in my legs from traveling up into my lungs. I later discovered that pulmonary embolisms are common among individuals who have recently suffered spinal cord injuries or anyone who has been sedentary for any considerable length of time.

Unfortunately, for most, this condition often results in immediate death. But, at the time, the procedure just seemed to be one of many unnecessary forms of sadistic practices that I would have to endure.

Another reason for the never-ending series of tests was to examine the position of the bullet. Yes, the bullet was still lodged in my spine. It had pierced my neck just below my right ear, crashed into my second cervical vertebrae, barely missing my brain stem. There it sat—a sinister souvenir—just inches away from my brain; and there it would stay for nearly nine more months. The doctors concluded that it would be far too dangerous to attempt to remove it. Wow, just the thought of that, gives me shivers; even many years later.

By all accounts, I could have, and probably, should have suffered severe brain damage, at the very least. If that bullet had been placed, just centimeters higher, I probably would not have survived. I certainly wouldn't have the capacity to write this, or anything else, for that matter.

SIDE EFFECTS

As a result, of this critical spinal cord injury, I had to receive treatment from a highly specialized trauma center with a uniquely trained team of medical personnel. This center treated all of the severely injured, high physical trauma patients in the DC/Baltimore metropolitan area. Many of the fellow patients were victims of violent attacks like gunshots and stabbings; also treated here were car accident victims who may have suffered spinal cord injuries and severe head trauma. Unfortunately, these sorts of occurrences were too common at this particular hospital. Too many times, I was awakened late at night by the sound of emergency teams whisking a new patient down the hallways of the hospital ward. The form of care provided there was highly intensive and yet, highly delicate. Mine, was no different.

During this time I had no motor or sensory function below my neck. Meaning, I could not move anything or feel anything below my level of injury. I couldn't breathe at all on my own, and I was restricted to the assistance of a ventilator that was placed beside my bed. This gargantuan machine pumped room air and filtered oxygen through a tube into my windpipe in order to inflate my lungs, because my diaphragm muscles couldn't. My spinal cord was torn at the C2 (second cervical vertebrae) region, so, every region of my spinal cord beneath that, and its corresponding functions, were affected. My digestion was severely limited, and so was my ability to excrete waste. I was restricted from eating any solid foods or drinking any fluids, whatsoever. The only nourishment I received was from a "feeding tube" that was inserted through my nose, down my esophagus, and into my stomach.

Considering my mental state during this time, it's understandable that this was a tough proposition for me to accept. The very idea of them inserting a tube inside of my nose was horrifying. Not understanding the purpose for that procedure, I was certain that this was again one of the many torture tactics assigned to be issued out by these strangers. Needless to say, I was completely uncooperative.

The environment that I found myself in during these early days was horrifying. I had no clue as to where I was, nor the reason I was being "held" there. I was never particularly fond of hospitals before, and had never really been inside of one, except to visit someone (like my very accident-prone brother, during our childhood days). But, I believe my confusion was a direct effect of the heavy dosage of medications I was receiving at the time. In fact, the confusion and fear that I felt at the time quickly elevated to a sense of constant paranoia.

I believe the toughest adjustment to make was having to go for a month or so without water. Granted, I was receiving the necessary amount of nutrients that my body needed from the feeding tube. But, the pain I felt from not being able to even take a sip of water was excruciating. I was only allowed to chew on a small damp sponge, occasionally, to moisten my mouth. I would literally beg my visitors to secretly give me a short drink of anything. I'm sure this was as equally difficult for them to handle, as well. They were not to give me any water—under any circumstances—per instruction of my doctors. Actually, this wasn't just another conspired form of "cruel and unusual" punishment; there was legitimate reason for this order. There was a high probability that any fluids taken by mouth could travel down the "wrong hole," so to speak, and into my lungs. Aspiration is a very harmful threat that often occurs with individuals who suffer injuries similar to mine.

The most difficult aspect, however, was the psychological toll that this had on me. Just imagine being deprived of water for a period of weeks; how difficult would that be for anyone to endure. This along with other treatments and precautions only fed my theory that there was some conspiracy formed against me.

That was only the beginning. My entire body was severely swollen, due to the severe shock my body suffered initially. It was difficult to assess the severity of my injuries, or determine how long these symptoms would persist, until the swelling around the region of my spinal cord subsided. At this point, my survival was still in question, but it was certain that difficult times were ahead.

In these early days following my injury, I suffered several setbacks that complicated my recovery process. One in particular was my development of a near fatal lung disorder: ARDS, (Acute Respiratory Distress Syndrome), a condition I was later informed, that kills nine out of 10 of those who are affected. This condition generated a large build-up of fluid in my lungs that was fairly difficult to treat. In order to treat this,

I had to spend each moment on a scary-looking device called a striker frame. This was a bed that rested on a swivel-like frame that allowed it to rotate upside down. Now, I had to remain on this day and night, for nearly a month. I had to be tightly strapped into this frame and flipped upside down for two hours at a time, around-the-clock. I had to lay their upside down, for a couple of hours at a time, in order to treat this buildup of fluid in my lungs. This was a very critical form of treatment that was essential to my survival. What was treatment in the doctor's viewpoint was torture from mine.

I have vivid memories of myself staring at the floor of the hospital room, for hours, completely distraught. It took a team of nurses and aides, to conduct this treatment. I dreaded to hear the convoy of personnel coming my way, because I knew what was coming next.

I was very fortunate, however, to have two very special friends to help me cope during this troubling time. Necole and Tress, two friends from the Baltimore area, would visit each and every day, and would take turns lying on the floor, to accompany me. They would, ceremoniously, come and lay in front of me as I was hanging from this contraption; and they would read to me or just converse with me, for hours. More times than not, I was completely unpleasant, and it showed.

So, I'm sure it was a difficult task for them, at times. But, I am grateful for their concern and level of commitment. It was considerably important at an awfully critical time; and I have never been able to express to them, just how important it was to me.

As I write this, I am reminded of one particular occasion that makes me chuckle every time I think about it. One day, (or night, I can't remember which) the crowd had come into my room to flip me upside down again, but, this time I was determined to prevent it from happening. Faced with having to stare at the floor for two straight hours, I needed to figure out a way to stop this, once and for all. I couldn't talk or move, but I managed to communicate to the staff that I needed my mother immediately. Reluctantly, they stopped the procedure, to summon my mom.

As she approached my bedside, the staff exited so that we could have our privacy. Then, she leaned closer and I mouthed the plea to "call the police, they are torturing me." She just smiled, and said, "OK, honey, I will get the police." This completely angered me, and supported my theory that everyone in that hospital was involved in some evil scheme against me. And now, my mother had been brainwashed, too.

In actuality, they were performing a procedure critical to my survival. As distressing and uncomfortable as it was, it was needed if I was going to stay alive. My misguided perception was attributed to the tremendous amount of shock that surrounded the injury, as well as the heavy dosage of medications that were being pumped into my system. I had to receive steroids intended to limit the damage to the spinal cord, pain medication, anti-anxiety medication, and sleeping pills; all were given to me, simultaneously. This hodgepodge of medications warped my understanding of where I was — and why I couldn't leave.

In my mind, I felt as if I was being imprisoned and held hostage in the hospital room. Despite all of the intensive medical procedures, and their resulting physical and emotional effects, I managed to survive with my spirit in tact.

Up to this point, I truly believed I was in some sort of prolonged dream, and furthermore, at any given moment, I would wake up, get out of that bed, and walk out of that hospital. However, one particular experience served as an epiphany to the overwhelming seriousness of my situation. This moment represented the low point of my hospital stay. It was this, the first time that I was placed into a wheelchair that challenged my willpower to an unbelievable extent.

This occurred approximately three weeks after my initial hospitalization. For three weeks I was forced to remain in that bed; unable to move anything, voluntarily. The only relief my body received was my occasional passive range of motion exercise routine (performed by a physical therapist); and when they would temporarily roll me onto my side to relieve pressure on my back.

Now, I had to face sitting upright for the first time in weeks. By then my body had completely adjusted to a sedentary, bed-ridden state, and any drastic changes in positioning would create harmful side effects. It is a difficult concept, I'm sure, especially if you have never experienced it before. But, getting in this chair for the first time was literally the most physically painful experience of my life. My blood pressure dropped drastically causing severe lightheadedness and probably the most excruciating headache in the history of mankind. My whole body completely rejected this move and screamed in pain. The pain was so intense that I could only withstand approximately five minutes in the chair, before begging for the staff to lay me down.

Before I could get into the bed, again, my eyes were completely flooded with tears. This was the very first time I had actually cried throughout this whole ordeal, which is somewhat surprising considering all that I had been through. In my mind, for a man to cry would be the ultimate sign of weakness. Maybe I, like many other young men, was more conditioned to believe this. Also, any display of emotion or vulnerability would somehow mean that I was losing this battle, and I was determined not to lose this battle. However, I must admit this idea is a complete lie that many young men deceive themselves into believing as true. Admittedly, I still have difficulty expressing significant emotion. In effect, what I was really doing to myself was limiting any healing process from taking place and not allowing myself to begin to make the necessary adjustments.

There was a buildup of anger, fear, frustration, etc.; so many negative emotions had been penned up inside of me — and erupted in that instance.

The physical pain was certainly a major factor, but, an equal contributor was my damaged psyche. Before this injury, I was a completely healthy, athletic young man who had never seen a significant injury in his lifetime. The extent of my history of injury, until then, was an occasional pulled muscle or sprained ankle. So, my mindset suffered a tremendous blow. Reality had officially "set in," and I then began to realize that difficult times were ahead. Before, I had completely refused to accept this reality and now I was forced to face it.

To a certain extent, I believe that it was important for me to not acquiesce to this calm state of acceptance, because I may not have survived those early stages. It is my belief that it takes a certain amount of stubbornness to overcome unbelievable, unthinkable, and unimaginable challenges. I thank God for this sort of fortitude, because it enabled me to fight off depression and suicidal thoughts, for that matter. I always believed with the utmost confidence that I could overcome any obstacles in front of me, but, this moment exposed my vulnerability. This was a completely different "beast," altogether; one that I couldn't defeat on my own. The little bit of perseverance or strength that I possessed wouldn't be enough to prevent my current circumstances from breaking my spirit. Without question, I knew that I needed Him now, more than ever before.

Shortly after this first experience in a wheelchair, I began to adjust physically. My body slowly became accustomed to sitting upright again as I would have to gradually increase the amount of time spent in the wheelchair each day. It was completely bewildering and embarrassing to me, just how gradual the time increments were. I believe we increased the requirements by one minute each day, and I counted every single second that passed. However, each moment, each second represented progress. Not to the extent to which I had envisioned, but it was progress, nonetheless.

The intense medical regimen persisted, though, as I was literally hanging in the balance "day by day." My condition remained critical for the next couple of weeks, until, one day I experienced a sudden and significant reversal in my condition, as well as my outlook.

Almost overnight, there was a drastic shift in my recovery. I awoke one morning feeling surprisingly vibrant and completely aware of my surroundings. I can imagine it being much like someone waking up after spending an expanded period of time in a coma. I don't believe that I ever quite slipped into a comatose state, but, I was plagued by periods of unconsciousness, as well as, sporadic bouts with hallucinations for nearly 90 days straight.

But, on this day, my condition suddenly changed and the focus of my medical team shifted from stabilizing me to rehabilitating me! Immediately they began to make plans to send me to a rehab center. More importantly for me, these improvements meant that I could eat again and get rid of that dreaded tube that had been hanging from my nose.

The excitement seemed to spread throughout the hospital. My medical team eagerly anticipated this moment, but many of them, I'm sure, doubted that it would ever arrive. Much of my "involuntary" function returned to my body, overnight.

Though, I was still nearly completely paralyzed, critical functionality (things most of us take for granted) returned to me, which was another sign of subtle, but significant, progress.

Because of the lack of nourishment I received during the first few weeks, I experienced a dramatic and dangerous loss in weight. My weight had dropped over 50 pounds in a matter of days, to around 130 lbs. Now, I was cleared to eat solid foods again because I had regained control of my ability to swallow... and boy, did I eat. I placed my orders: everything from Chinese, seafood, to various forms of junk food; and every nurse in that hospital obliged me. I was soon surrounded by a buffet of my choosing and I tried to devour every bit of it. As a testament to too much of a good thing, I stuffed myself so much, that I became terribly sick and was forced to fast again for a couple of days. Live and learn...

Even though I overindulged in food—and paid severely for it—this point in time marked a turning point in my journey. Medically, this was really the first sign of optimism toward my recovery. This optimism began to circulate among everyone around me, even among the doctors who previously doubted that I would even live through this.

However, just as things began to "look up," tragedy struck again.

Ms. Patterson:
In hospital settings such as this, medical personnel, family, and friends, alike, all rally together and support one another. In the midst of tragic circumstances, a loving atmosphere is created wherein everyone involved becomes unified in the common hope of restoring the injured or sick patient. Oftentimes, an extended family is created among people who have never seen each other before and may have come from completely different backgrounds. My situation was no different. One person, in particular, emerged as a considerable source of love and support to my mother during these difficult times.

She was a hospital clerk who worked on my floor during evening hours. She was fairly young, probably in her late twenties. Ms. Patterson, as I recall (I can't remember her first name), was an awfully nice, generous woman. She was a tremendous benefit to the patients and their families, of that particular ward. Nearly every night, she would sit at my bedside and converse with me; often during those lonely, depressing nights that were all too common. She would often take my mother out for lunch, coffee, or just a comforting walk around downtown Baltimore; which provided a much-needed escape for my mom who was experiencing such a tough time.

She had become very dear to my mother and me, as well as, to other patients and co-workers. Ms. Patterson was one of those people whose warmth and vibrancy radiated throughout the atmosphere, and her presence illuminated the environment around her.

But, one morning I awoke to be met with some terrible news. The atmosphere was heavy and the mood of the other hospital workers was noticeably solemn. I immediately recognized that something was wrong by the unusual demeanors and the look on the faces of the hospital staff that morning. So I began to inquire of others as to what was going on. One hospital aide, who was a close friend of Ms. Patterson's, reluctantly informed me that she had been murdered on the previous night. The report from her was that Ms. Patterson and a friend were found dead in their car with gunshot wounds to the back of their heads!

This news, obviously, was very troubling to me along with everyone in that hospital who had gotten to know Ms. Patterson. It was unbelievable for any of us to fathom. Why would anyone want to hurt such a sweet individual? This was a tremendous shock to those who were close to her, and understandably so. Although, I had only known her for a short period of time, I shared in their grief. I would be remiss in failing to mention this most unfortunate tragedy. I am sure she is missed terribly. I don't know the status of her case but, I hope that it wasn't "swept under the rug," like my case was— and many others in that particular region. I'm sure her memory and valuable legacy continues on among many of those who were blessed to know her.

But, for the brief time I knew her, she made an indelible impact on me. While deciding to undertake the task of writing this book, I determined in myself to give some sort of tribute to this person; though her memory deserves much more than this. However, I do believe that there is much to be learned from that experience. Her legacy may not extend into the far reaches of our planet, and probably won't receive annual tribute. But, her legacy nonetheless is just as significant as those who do receive such honor. As a hospital clerk, she was somewhat isolated from the patients and their families. Also, that position requires that they limit their contact with the patients and not get personally involved in any aspects of their treatment. But, she took it upon herself to proactively show her concern and support for my family and I, throughout this ordeal. She didn't have to, but she devoted herself to comforting others in need. Isn't that the sort of impact we should all strive to make?

As I am writing this, many specific details, which I probably suppressed for years or simply forgot about, come to mind. I remember that there was a tremendous wave of support and concern from those who heard of my unfortunate incident. So many individuals extended themselves and rallied in support of myself and my family. Much of the news media, the hundreds of letters that poured in, and the many visitations from friends and complete strangers, as well; they all represented the same character that I witnessed in Ms. Patterson. There is one visitation, I can recall, that was very significant in building my resolve, early on. At a time when I was completely overwhelmed by fear and confusion, I received a source of needed inspiration, in the form of a stranger.

This particular day, I believe it was the Saturday or Sunday afternoon following the shooting. It was a time when I was experiencing periodic lapses of consciousness and my moments of awareness were few and far between. This time I awoke to see an orderly standing in my room. Because of the state of mind I was in, I believed that I was being imprisoned in this hospital room, against my will. And for the life of me, I couldn't understand why. I don't know exactly what he was doing, but, he appeared to be restocking some medical supplies. Although he probably was unaware of my entire set of circumstances, I proceeded to ask him for some explanation as to what was going on. However, the only words that I could gather were, "can you help me?"

The young man stared at me for a moment, and then said, "no, I can't do anything for you," and then he walked away. I am confident that he had no intentions of being cruel, nevertheless this was damaging to me. But, I believe my cries were more for answers, during a very horrifying and confusing moment, rather than for any sort of physical assistance.

Next, I remember laying there, for what seemed like hours, just staring at the wall in front of me, wondering where I was, who were these strange people, and where was my family? Then suddenly, a woman eased her way into my room and began to talk to me.

Now, I did know that it wasn't visiting hours and this woman was wearing civilian clothing. So, she wasn't part of the hospital staff. She approached my bedside and gave me some very inspiring words. She mentioned, that she "knew my brother," and wanted to pray with me. How she managed to get past hospital "security" during non-visiting hours, was astounding to me. But, how did she know my older brother who, months before my injury, had joined a seminary school in Texas?

My brother, Brent, and I, were never very close because we were always distantly located from each other, and we had not talked for months prior to this incident.

However, she asked if she could pray with me, and I agreed. She prayed for my healing, protection, and that God would just reside with me throughout this ordeal. As soon as we finished praying together, she seemed to disappear. This experience came at a moment in time that was awfully critical. I was completely devastated at this time, because the reality of my harsh circumstances had just begun to set in. The confusion and fear completely overwhelmed me. I had no clue as to where I was or why I couldn't leave. And when I reached out for help from the orderly, he presumably, turned his back on me and walked away.

Understand, this was one of my first fully conscious moments since arriving in Baltimore. Until then, I was in a comatose-like state, constantly drifting in and out of awareness (mainly due to the masses of medications and the tremendous shock of the injury itself). I felt completely abandoned. The waves of support that were building outside of the hospital and up-and-down the entire East Coast were not apparent to me, hence, the reason that the timing was so critical. Just when I was about to "throw in the towel," God sent someone to intervene. Probably, more important than that, was the fact that she responded.

Similar visitations such as this are common in hospital settings; where "missionaries" seek out opportunities to encourage and comfort the sick and injured. There were many occasions similar to this that occurred throughout my lengthy hospital stay, however, this particular visit remains fixed in my memory bank. Perhaps it was because it was one of the first "friendly" faces that I saw, or maybe it was the near-perfect timing of the event. Nevertheless, this somewhat strange encounter had a profoundly positive effect on me. But,

I believe that the recount of this incident provides a crucial example for us all. In our daily lives, there are numerous opportunities to encourage and uplift the lives of others; opportunities that we often overlook. Most times hurting individuals don't wear a sign expressing their particular pain; in fact, most of us who are hurting go to considerable lengths to conceal it. But deep inside, most people are screaming and hoping for someone to take interest. The simplicity of compassion is that most often, it only requires a small gesture of concern. A simple smile or words of encouragement go further than we often realize.

This was one of many examples of a completely selfless concern for others that I experienced throughout my hospital stay and in the years since (all of which, I am completely grateful for). They all have served as a tremendous lesson for me throughout this journey. I have learned of the overwhelming significance that gestures like these have on the lives of suffering individuals — and that I am not exempt from the responsibility to act accordingly. I thank God for all of those people, including those classmates, local dignitaries, and certainly my family members, who all reached out on my behalf. I would certainly need every ounce of encouragement during the days that lay ahead.

The news of my injury had begun to spread throughout my home state. Now friends, family, and classmates who were certainly concerned, but completely uninformed of my medical status started to flock toward Baltimore. Media reports of the shooting had flooded the airwaves in North Carolina and the entire eastern coast. This created a flood of concern and interest in my well-being from those with whom I had affiliations, as well as, complete strangers who were genuinely moved by the circumstances involved. The level of response and the wave of support that erupted were enormous. I, for the most part, was oblivious to what was going on during this time. But, it was a tremendous blessing to see the faces of my closest friends and family members, when I did occasionally rise into consciousness.

Despite the overwhelming support that poured in for my family and me, I was forced to cope with the most unbelievable set of circumstances that anyone could imagine facing. The three of us (my friends and I), found ourselves in the middle of this vicious attack that took place for no legitimate reason, whatsoever. This attack, one that easily could have ended all of our lives, left me nearly completely paralyzed; but, all of us were left emotionally wounded. Those scars don't ever completely heal.

At this point, I had experienced a lifetime of hardships, both physical and emotional, as a result of what happened that night. During the first two months following the attack, I experienced countless numbers of disappointments and setbacks, sprinkled with very few victories and positives. The most difficult stage of my new life was behind me. I had somehow survived unimaginable circumstances. I had survived the shooting and a world of physical complications beyond all medical reason and expectation. There was a bleak light of optimism shining over my life now, and in retrospect, this period of time represented a tremendous time of progress toward recovery in every sense.

CHAPTER 4: NEW JERSEY: What's Next?

Approximately three months had passed since that night, that horrible night that nearly meant the end for me; and certainly turned my life upside down. It was still unclear as to what would lie ahead, but considering the grueling, painful moments that were behind me, nothing could possibly be as bad, so I thought.

I was surprisingly upbeat and optimistic as I took that two hour ambulance ride from Baltimore to my next destination, Kessler Institute of Rehabilitation in West Orange, New Jersey. Somewhat fearful of the unknown challenges and circumstances surrounding the next phase of my rehabilitation, I began to adopt the belief that I would overcome whatever came my way.

Upon my arrival at Kessler rehab, I quickly began to feel fearful and uncertain about my new surroundings. Even though my condition had drastically changed for the better, which allowed me to be transferred to a center of rehabilitation, I had grown accustomed to the people and content with the quality of care that I receive in Baltimore. That environment had become safe and familiar to me.

Also frightening, I seemed to be migrating farther and farther away from home; away from my friends and family in North Carolina. Fortunately, we were well aware of the center's reputation of excellent care for new spinal cord patients. It also helped that I had several caring family members in the New York/New Jersey area. So, as terrifying as it was for me, I had to continue forward!

The first night there was pretty much uneventful. I was lifted into my bed in my own room, which I was fortunate to have, because the majority of patients were forced to share a room like this with two or three others. This would turn out to be blessing for me because the isolation would allow me to have "personal time" with God in those critical moments. During those moments of depression and discouragement, that were all too often, I was free to pray, and to just speak with Him, free from distraction and interruption. Those moments allowed me to receive His peace and comfort throughout those frequent lonely, depressing nights.

It is my belief that this was critical to my survival because, during these moments of despair, I could have someone play the tape with the Bible or inspirational music on it. In those moments, where I felt like I was under some sort of psychological attack, I could have a clear channel to the Father.

One of my first encounters with another patient in the hospital occurred during one of those early nights in the rehab center. Shortly after settling into this new environment, the man who resided in the hospital room adjacent to mine slowly steered his wheelchair into my room. He obviously wanted to offer some encouragement to the newest arrival. This man was Christopher Reeve—the renowned and accomplished actor who's most tragic, unfortunate accident had occurred only months before mine.

He approached my bedside and offered some encouraging words to me. The encounter only lasted for 30 minutes or so, but, one statement that he made really stood out. He said, "It looks like we are in the same boat." This statement and the meeting itself, though seemingly insignificant, was a tremendous motivator for me.

This meeting gave me a different perspective on what I was faced with. Even though it had been more than two months since the shooting occurred, Chris was really the first person who I had any contact with who had an injury similar to mine. Until then, I felt as if I was the only person on the planet in this situation.

Though our other encounters were brief and relatively less profound, they gave me a new perspective on my situation and the apparent struggles ahead. I had finally met someone who could relate and identify with my trials. At that moment, I realized that there were many others, from all sectors of society, facing the same battle. We were, in fact, in the "same boat." We were forced to fight an unimaginable, uninvited enemy who had invaded and nearly destroyed everything.

Helping individuals come to terms with their situation is primarily what spinal cord centers such as the one in New Jersey are designed to do; to initiate associations with others with similar struggles and to promote re-integration into society and a "normal" life.

I have come to learn that God often positions people to assist us in like fashion and critical moments. People are placed in our paths, sometimes briefly, just to encourage and assist us to reach that next step, along the way. This encounter served that function in that phase of my recovery. I admire and respect the work that Chris went on to do. He had successfully managed to bring about awareness to the world of spinal cord injury and disease, and in effect, provided a voice for a group of people who never really had one.

In fact, there are many others in that hospital who extended themselves to provide inspiration throughout the following three months of my stay. For in those next three months would come the most physically demanding days of my recovery.

I immediately recognized the change in the level of care in this hospital; not so much in the quality of care, but, the intensity of care that I received dramatically increased. Before, in Baltimore, the atmosphere was much more "relaxed." My day actually began in the early afternoon due to the large amounts of medications I was receiving that were intended to induce rest. Besides, the majority of that time was spent saving my life and stabilizing me, rather than focusing on recuperation. At this point, the difference had become obvious.

My first days resembled that of a new military recruit entering boot camp for the first time, and my nurses were the drill sergeants. At the first sign of daybreak, they would march into my room and turn on every light and open every curtain in sight. Needless to say, I wasn't very fond of this practice or any of its participants—namely the nurses. However, I slowly realized how fortunate I was to have a team of caregivers who wouldn't give me a break, and that would push me relentlessly toward my path to recovery. I had no time or energy to feel sorry for myself.

After my early-morning wakeup call, my nurses would perform various general health assessments, blood-pressure checks, oxygen saturations, etc., followed by a quick exercise routine and sponge bath. From there, I was lifted into my wheelchair and wheeled away to a spinal cord education class which began at 9:00 a.m. daily. The class itself was a very helpful experience for new spinal cord patients. This particular class served two beneficial functions. First, the instructors of the course were to quell the overwhelming fears and concerns that many spinal cord patients face in the early stages of their new life. There were individuals suffering from various forms of spinal cord injury, from gunshot wounds to car accidents to stroke. However, we all shared common concerns.

What was next? Would our conditions improve? How soon? How much longer? What now?

In essence, the class dealt with the psychological adjustments that needed to be made, which in turn, would eventually assist us with re-integration back into society when our rehab stint was over?

Second, the course was designed to educate us on the many physical dynamics related to the various spinal cord injuries that were represented. For me, I was facing complete paralysis; so, every single system of my body and the related functions, were affected (or limited). This portion of the class was to make the patients aware of all aspects of their physical care. They vehemently stressed its importance.

They believed that each patient in that hospital should have complete understanding of his/her injury (or disease) and the many intricacies involving the conditions and its treatments. Their goal was to provide enough information so that the patients would be able to instruct a complete stranger, with no medical background, how to provide any sort of care or assistance they may need.

I have come to realize that this is a very critical aspect of rehabilitation for individuals with spinal cord injuries, and it is an aspect that is often neglected. This form of instruction can, and oftentimes does, prevent possible complications.

I was a terrible student. The overall theme of the spinal cord classes was to help patients with acceptance of their new reality and the resulting adjustments that needed to be made. I had a tremendous amount of trouble accepting this as my fate (even now, I refuse to accept it), so, understandably I rejected any ideas of conform.

To me, everyone else, who seemed to have accepted this reality, had simply just given up. "I will walk out of this hospital, completely recovered," I constantly reminded myself. This is what I truly believed and I wouldn't allow anything else to penetrate or "poison" this belief. I recognize now, that such a belief was completely unsuitable because of the undeniable benefit of that education, but it describes my mindset at the time. Instead, I was more interested in the physical therapy sessions because they were much more beneficial to accomplishing that goal.

Each day, following those classes we preceded to the gym for occupational and physical therapy sessions. Each session lasted a couple of hours, and they ran consecutively throughout the day.

The occupational therapy sessions were geared toward teaching patients how to work with various forms of adaptive technology, like computers, power wheelchairs, etc.

The physical therapy, on the other hand, was an intense, physically demanding experience, each and every day. I received electrical stimulation to every muscle in my body, it seemed, for prolonged periods of time. This procedure was designed to tests my muscle response and to reverse muscle atrophy in the arms and legs. This was terribly important because of the extended amount of time since the shooting that I had actually been unable to "move a muscle" in my body. As a result, I had lost a tremendous amount of muscle tone and definition, and my body was completely frail. So, the electro-stimulation was extremely helpful.

Another form of physical therapy that I received was the dreaded "standing table." This table resembled some mechanical monstrosity you would find in a classic horror movie. My therapists would lift me onto this flat table, strap me in this thing from head to toe, and raise it up into a vertical position. Its purpose was threefold: 1) The procedure helped to promote circulation, which decreased the common threat of blood clotting; 2) It was to help maintain bone density in the legs. For anyone who is bedridden for any amount of time, the loss of bone density due to calcium deposits, is a common occurrence. 3) Also, this treatment helps to restore the standing equilibrium in the body. It was designed to train the body to adjust to an upright position.

This seems like a minor, simple task, but it was the most difficult aspect of my physical therapy program. When the body becomes so accustomed to lying flat, as mine was, any attempts to sit upright or stand causes drastic changes in blood-pressure. The physical therapists would turn a crank mounted to the side of the bed to gradually raise me up, and each time I would experience the most excruciating pain I have ever felt in my life. My blood-pressure would plummet, and I would feel extremely lightheaded at the slightest increases in the angle of my positioning.

After the few hours of these intense therapy sessions, everyone headed toward the cafeteria for lunch; everyone except for me. I would always pass by the cafeteria, straight into my bedroom. Rather than join the others in the cafeteria, where I would be forced to communicate, I chose to spend this time alone in my room before I had to resume my physical therapy. I did this partly because of the unfamiliarity surrounding me, as well as, the anxiety that I felt from my increased self-consciousness and diminished self-esteem.

On top of that, many other patients in that hospital, who had suffered similar tragedies as mine, were suffering from severe depression. As a result, suicide attempts were all too common there. The vast majority of rehab patients were upbeat and optimistic about their future; however, there was still a lingering cloud of despair over the lives of several of the patients. Unfortunately, I heard a number of accounts of suicidal plans had been circulating throughout the center. So, to prevent similar ideas from penetrating my own psyche, I chose not to associate with most of the others. This sort of displacement was a defense mechanism that was designed to shield my system of beliefs from any form off negativity.

I was determined to walk out of that hospital, and I didn't want anything to discourage me or impede that confidence. But, in retrospect, had I decided to spend more time with the others, my experience at Kessler would have been much more enjoyable. I later learned that most of the patients were as helpful and optimistic as I was, and by responding this way I denied myself of some potentially meaningful relationships with several wonderful people. Nevertheless, this is how I coped with this overwhelming situation that I was in at the time. Fortunately, I had a team of dedicated caregivers who extended themselves to help me when things got tough.

Besides the excellent treatment I received at this, a top-flight rehabilitation center, the staff turned out to be some of the most generous, helpful people that I have ever come in contact with, in my life. As time went on, I came to develop close friendships with several of the staff members. The complete staff, from the physicians down, was completely supportive of my family and me. I couldn't begin to name everyone because there were so many who made an impact during those crucial times (and for fear that I may forget someone). But, some of them, like Doctors Green and Kirsch Bloom, Sandy, Serita, Elaine, Meredith, Ozzie, "Juice," and Charles, to name a few, were all important to my success there. Two of my therapists in particular, were significant figures in my emotional adjustment to my new life.

Faced with overwhelming fear and anxiety, I was completely intimidated by my surroundings. It is awfully difficult for me to illustrate the level of anxiety that one, who was in my situation, experiences. At night, I would stare at the ventilator, which was placed beside my bed pumping air through a tube into my lungs, for hours, just hoping that it wouldn't "pop off." These nights were spent in perpetual fear that I would lose my air supply and no one would hear the alarm sounding; or the often depressing moments when friends of mine would visit and bear witness to my new, unfortunate condition, for the first time. These are just illustrations of the intensity of the fears I experienced.

Circumstances like these contributed to a paralyzing fear that, at times, overwhelmed me and would nearly contribute to severe psychological breakdown. The social anxiety also was tremendously difficult for me to overcome. This is probably the primary reason for my avoidance of any significant contact with the other patients.

My two therapists, Elaine and Sandy, put considerable effort into helping me adjust. My mentality was certainly not unusual, and the professionals at this center were highly successful with breaking these barriers. They always managed to lift my spirits and make me laugh, even when laughter was the last thing on my mind. They were a group of dedicated individuals who poured their heart into their work. They made a tremendous impact on me, as well as many others in that hospital.

In retrospect, I am tremendously grateful for that experience. Not, the entire set of circumstances, namely the injury itself, which I could have done without. But in my most vivid memories, I can recall one minor point of my experience in West Orange that really stands out in my mind.

Early on, during my stay at Kessler, some of my family members from the area visited me. My cousin, Uchee, who was around 10 years old at the time, brought a poster she had designed for me to hang on my wall. This poster had a bunch of colorful designs on its border, with flowers and little animals throughout. It also contained a passage of scripture in the center that would provide a great deal of inspiration for me, during those fearful, lonely nights. The poster that was placed on the wall directly in front of me, read:

> *But those who [b]wait on the LORD*
> *[c]Shall renew their strength;*
> *They shall mount up with wings like eagles,*
> *They shall run and not be weary,*
> *They shall walk and not faint. (Isaiah 40: 31, NKJ)*

Even though I would rarely admit to it—and even fought endlessly to conceal the fact—I was suffering a great deal of emotional pain at this time. My beliefs, as well as the defenses that had been erected prevented me from confessing this fact. But, I was in the middle of an emotional whirlwind. Everywhere I turned I saw nothing but despair. I would often experience moments of contentment and inspiration (that would linger only momentarily) from the many visits, phone calls, and letters that I received during this time, but, at the end of the night, I would look at the circumstances and constantly be reminded of my "horrific" position.

During these times I needed something to rekindle the positive outlook and optimism that was already within. It was a small gesture, seemingly, but, it had a resounding effect.

This poster and the message contained served as a souvenir constantly reminding me of what my goals were and exactly how I would achieve them. From the very moment my injury occurred, I placed my trust and confidence solely in God. I also knew that it was God who moved so miraculously to save my life. Furthermore, since medical science provided no hope for my recovery, then God would have to do it. This passage reminded me that I would have to exercise patience; that I was going to persevere, that I should not rely on my own strength but rely on Him, and if I did so, only then could I soar above the unbelievable challenges in front of me.

Even more so, the language used in this particular text appealed mostly to me. Since my ultimate goal was to stand, walk, and run again, then by exhibiting these characteristics I would be strengthened in my anxious, but confident expectation of their fruition. As my hope was being worked out for me, I could withstand these daily battles. This note served as my daily reminder and one of my constant motivators. A simple gesture by a little girl had a resounding impact on my daily affirmation; one that she was probably never aware of.

In fact, it is gestures like this, the ones that go unnoticed, unannounced that are the most rewarding and that have the most impact. They seem to be the most genuine, sincere acts of kindness. These kinds of expressions were so prominent in the recounts of my hospital stay, in Maryland and New Jersey. The hospitals staffs, and the many friends and family, and the many concerned individuals who took the time to write letters or send cards, were all instrumental to my survival early on. All of which, I am tremendously grateful for.

So resoundingly evident, also, was the critical presence of my mother throughout this entire experience. She was there from day one, providing the comfort that I most urgently needed. She placed her entire life on hold in order to be by my side. For this I am completely and utterly grateful.

Equally as important and noticeable, was that God was always there with me, right beside me. He was present when the attack occurred, when I hopelessly lay their in the ER, even during those frequent lonely nights, to comfort me when I couldn't find any. He rescued me from death, sustained me throughout, and provided the strength that I needed to endure. The worst of the physical complications were behind me; and now I was faced with a new, equal set of challenges in front of me. And now I would need Him more than ever.

Author Gregory Allen Patterson with parents Cathy and Gary at a family member's wedding in Greensboro, NC.

Cousins Keith Patterson (l) and Gregory Allen Patterson (r) enjoying some free time during Spring Break at Myrtle Beach, SC in 1992.

Brothers Phillip and Gregory Allen Patterson during their years in the "minor leagues."

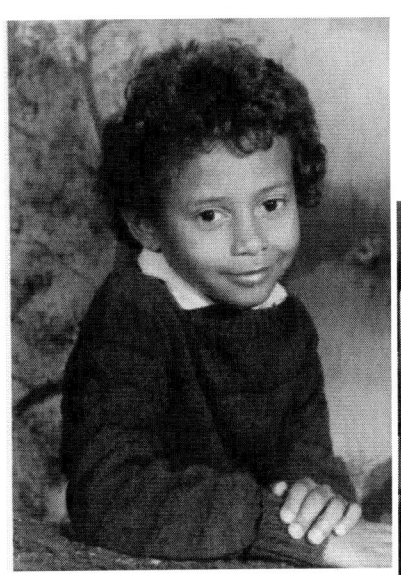

Gregory Allen Patterson in 1st grade at Cone Elementary School in Greensboro, NC.

Gregory Allen Patterson poses with cousin and groom-to-be Keith Patterson (l) and co-best man/brother Tony Patterson (r) in 1999.

Gregory Allen Patterson
September 29, 1976 ~ November 21, 2005

CHAPTER 5: JOURNEY HOME: *Home Sweet Home!*

A new phase of my life was about to begin. What started out initially as a short leisure trip—a pleasant deviation from the normal routine of college life—turned out to be a complete life-altering set of experiences for me. In the five months of recovery, I experienced several lifetimes of experiences. Those days were marked with many victories and disappointments, losses and gains. Despite the horrible circumstances that I found myself in, I knew that I was fortunate. Fortunate to have had the team of caregivers around me who fought for me, with me, and beside me. But in all honesty, I had grown sick of hospital life and grown more desperate to return home.

It was early in the morning on March 5, 1996, when the call came for me to catch the plane destined for home. We were ecstatic at this news. I knew that I would miss many of the staff whom I had developed close friendships with during my stay. But, I also knew that my time there had run its course. I wasn't seeing any improvements in my physical condition, and my mind had long been fixated on my home in North Carolina.

I had reached a plateau in my recovery phase and had not experienced the dramatic improvements I hoped and was convinced would have occurred by that time. Yes, I had surpassed all initial expectations regarding my survival and recovery from these difficult circumstances, but, I fully expected to walk out of that rehab center wholly and completely restored.

Sure, there was disappointments because this hope had not come in to fruition at that point, but I had recognized that a change in locale would further these goals, and I had been earnestly praying and expecting. In settings like this, when a patient wants to go home, then he is probably stable enough to do so. It's his time. So, we said all of our goodbyes to the staff and fellow patients. Then, I was loaded onto a stretcher and carried outside to an ambulance waiting to take me to the airport.

The trip from the hospital to the airport lasted about one hour. Actually, the "airport" was a tiny runway strip in some deserted field in central New Jersey. Nevertheless, it was the most anxious, anticipated hour-long trip of my life. My eagerness turned into a paralyzing fear when we arrived and saw this airplane.

This airplane, which was used primarily for medical purposes (to transport ambulatory patients), was seemingly the size of a giant SUV.

What heightened the feelings of anxiety was the fact that I had never been on an airplane before. Nowadays, it's rare to see anyone over the age of 18 to never have boarded an airplane, but it was true. The passengers on this trip included the pilot, a nurse, a respiratory therapist, my mother, and me. We all piled into this miniature plane bound for home.

The flight lasted for approximately three hours and was rocky, to say the least. Somewhere near the midway point of the flight we encountered a tremendous amount of turbulence. When this happened, the plane shook beyond belief. Again, this was the very first time I had ever been on an airplane flight, so such turbulence was a completely new and nerve-wracking experience for me.

As everyone knows, the first time you experience major turbulence can be frightening. Because of my physical condition and the heightened sense of vulnerability that was related, I felt much more fearful. My first thought was that "I have just survived all of that trauma and complication, and now I am going down in a plane" But thankfully, we arrived safely at our destination. Thank God for big and small miracles.

As the plane touched down at Piedmont Triad International (PTI) airport in my hometown of Greensboro, NC, we were greeted by an overwhelming sight. There waiting by the runway were dozens of my family members accompanied by many of the local media. They all were there to welcome me as I was carried off of the plane and into an ambulance, waiting to take me home. I greeted my friends and family that were present, and I even tried to give an interview. I'm certain that watching the reporters attempting to shove microphones into a crowded ambulance had to be an amusing sight.

The ambulance sped away from the crowded airport — heading toward home. Directly behind us, were the vehicles full of reporters and photojournalists, attempting to beat the ambulance to my mother's home in order to get a photo opportunity of us entering the house. I couldn't see it from my positioning, but I can remember the paramedics beside me, laughing at the media blitz that my arrival home had caused.

Once we arrived at the street where my home stood, we were amazed to see that the whole street had been blocked off, preventing any traffic from floating by the enormous media scene surrounding our home. Cameras were everywhere!

I never quite understood the reasons for the media attention surrounding the whole incident; neither could I grasp the enormity of interest surrounding my situation—from that fateful night on the highway to the Baltimore hospital room, to the New Jersey rehab facility, to that very moment. To me, this was a "hero's" welcome, one that should have been given to a soldier coming home from a lengthy, perilous battle. I was certainly not worthy of such fanfare, I thought, however, I was certainly appreciative. I was grateful that the situation had not gone completely unnoticed.

Nonetheless, we survived the media frenzy and managed to get inside of the house. Then, I was carried on a stretcher into my bedroom that was prepared for me, and lifted onto my new bed.

From there, I continued to greet the many visitors that came by and take phone calls from friends and family throughout the evening. The reception was incredibly wonderful and was completely crucial to my already unstable morale. But, as wonderful as the reception was, I still had mixed feelings about arriving back home.

I had spent a considerable amount of time with people who had helped me through the most difficult life-changing event of my life—most of whom I had developed close bonds with. Now, I was undergoing another drastic change in my life. I was now forced to view life from a completely different lens. Even though I was in familiar settings with familiar people, nothing seemed quite the same.

ADJUSTMENTS

As I began my gradual adjustment to life at home, very little was actually familiar which made this adjustment much more difficult. In this sort of transition phase, one tends to search in painstaking fashion for any form of familiarity. The search itself is often a scary experience. Though I can only imagine what the experience is truly like, I liken such an experience similar to that of an individual stricken with amnesia and suddenly unfamiliar with his most familiar surroundings.

In some regards, this describes much of my perception during the early days of my return home. Sure, I was surrounded by many, many familiar faces and a great number of unfamiliar, but equally concerned individuals. However, I struggled to find the comfort that usually characterizes the term "home." Obviously, my life wasn't the same, and neither were the once-familiar aspects of what I called home.

A thousand questions floated around in my mind. What do I do now? How will people receive me? How long will I be like this? How long will I feel this way? These were some of the confusing questions that lingered inside of me and haunted my thoughts, severely hampering this otherwise festive occasion.

Again, my re-integration into my home environment and society was gradual. Days passed before I could appreciate the subtleties of life at home. But this revelation progressed when I received my first home-cooked meal. This significant aspect of my life had been absent from mine for far too long. I had spent the previous six months eating various forms of fast food, and even worse, hospital food. But, these home-cooked meals were usually prepared by my mother and my dear friend, Jeniel. I don't remember exactly what the menus were, but they helped me to forget that I missed New Jersey. It was moments like those, as well as other simple pleasures, that helped speed up the transition back to life at home.

I could now visit parks, shopping malls, and restaurants, or just stay at home and watch the game with my friends. All of these things—simple things—I often took for granted in the years prior to my near-fatal injury. Previously, while in New Jersey, I only went outdoors twice during a span of three months (mainly because of the record-breaking blizzard that destroyed the Tri-state area that winter).

Now, I was developing a new appreciation for the small things. Also, my personal outlook was positive, optimism was rising, and my friendships were, for the most part, productive and thriving.

The atmosphere throughout my home was a consistently festive and loving one. It seemed as if there was an extended celebratory mood that permeated throughout my home, my life, and everyone who was close to me. My whole family, it seemed, was a part of this celebratory spirit. We, as a family, have always been a tight, close-knit group. Everyone rallied together in support of my mother, brother, and me, and it was good to know how strong my support system was.

I believe that the most impressive and critical aspect of this whole scenario was that most, if not all, of my family members drew closer to God as a result of this tragic experience. The shooting served as a wakeup call for many of them, as well as, many others with whom I have come in contact with. 1 John 4 says that "God *is love*." This doesn't necessarily describe an attribute of God, but more so, it explains His essence. He is the creator of this emotion. So, where He is present, so is love. And all the people around me responded with love.

The response from my family and friends exemplified the unmistakable presence of God in all of our lives throughout the entire ordeal. They gave their time and energy to assist us in so many ways. They organized fund raisers to assist with the astronomical (and sometimes unfair) cost of equipment and supplies; they gave their prayers, and they gave their time to encourage and to accompany me when I needed it—as did the whole community. On a daily basis I would entertain the many friends and visitors—known and unknown—who would often visit me and be thrilled to see that I was "alive and well."

This was a typical routine for me for the first couple of years after returning home from the hospitals. It started to become evident to me that what seemed like a tragedy in the beginning wasn't really a tragedy at all. It was apparent that God used this "unfortunate" incident to positively affect the lives of those around me. He seemed to have used my misfortune to bring out the best in those around me. There is a biblical passage that, through these experiences, began to come alive right before my eyes:

28 †*We know that **all** things work for good for those who love God,* †*who are called according to his purpose (Romans 8: 28, NKJ).*

Honestly, from the very moment the shooting occurred, I failed to see any good in my circumstances. I knew that God had moved supernaturally and rescued me—beyond any medical reason or expectation. However, at the beginning I couldn't see any benefit from this tragic state of affairs.

This benefit that I heard so many others speak of was an illusion to me, until then. But this passage of scripture gave some insight on how God sees potential in situations that we view as unfortunate. He desires to turn our misfortunes around for our benefit, and more importantly, to positively impact the lives of others. In other words, He doesn't sulk at our calamities as we often do. Instead He is more focused on giving us the provisions we need and the healing we desire, from the inside out.

I viewed my paralysis as an unwelcome enemy who had invaded my camp, and I was going to drive him out by any means necessary. I intensely believed (and still do) that the same God who rescued me and sustained me, will also completely restore me.

Each day, I lived in expectancy that at any moment I would step out of that wheelchair that was restraining me. I knew that medicine offered no help for me, at the time. So, He would have to do it. Each day, I attacked my life with these things in mind. Most of my concentration was on my physical therapy routine because of the desire that was in me to walk again. So much so, I often totally neglected my social adaptations, that I since found were equally as important. As a result, I lost the friendships of several very important people — because I didn't allow myself to reciprocate the same love and concern that was given to me.

Unfortunately, I abandoned these people, which I truly regret.

On the other hand, maybe I needed that sort of focus, to some extent. In order to cope with the emotional pain resulting from the overwhelming change that had overtaken me and intense battles that were ahead, I needed no distractions. In fact, I strongly believe that this aggressive mindset helped to keep me from a complete emotional breakdown, during what had become a long, arduous road to recovery.

Shortly after I arrived at home from New Jersey, I slowly began to settle into my new/old surroundings. Instead of "crashing" at my mother's house for the weekend or on holidays, I was now there in a completely different capacity. It was now evident that I would be there for the major extent of my battle. Understandably, the circumstances concerning my health were completely different than before and still unfamiliar, which made for an awfully difficult adjustment.

Now, I was completely dependent on others for all of my physical and medical needs. Such dependence was completely foreign to me. Actually, I had always been the complete opposite; a confident, self-assured, and independent young man.

My day usually began with an exercise routine, breakfast, and then a bath; all of which had to be performed with the total assistance of someone else. Then, we usually followed this routine with a couple of hours spent with other physical therapy exercises like electrical muscle stimulation or the standing table. Then, we always repeated this routine at night, before going to sleep. Each and every step in the process was, and still is, a difficult and exhausting procedure.

A simple sponge bath, or just simply getting dressed, was a workout in itself.

The constant twisting and turning involved would absolutely exhaust me. But, I viewed all of it as a necessary means to the end I was hoping for. So, I remained very enthusiastic about every aspect of my life and routine, during this stage.

The overwhelming presence of fear still lingered around me. This fear, of unfamiliar territory, though I was completely unaware of it, stifled me for an extended period of time. Because of it, I was completely frightened of social situations. Oftentimes, weeks would go by without me leaving my home. Frightened and ashamed of my physical condition, I refused to allow myself to enjoy life because of this anxiety. The looks and stares that were frequent in public places completely discomfited me, so I stayed home as much as possible.

I'm sure that many of the looks I received were as much looks of concern and even compassion as they were astonishment or curiosity. Nevertheless, I perceived them to be jeers of contempt and negativity, which had a stifling effect on my life.

It is most unfortunate that many of the physically disabled experience similar anxieties on a daily basis. I believe it is our collective responsibility, whether we are completely healthy or otherwise, to extend concern and respect to individuals fighting or living with physical disabilities.

This perpetual state of fear plagued my life for most of the early years, following my injury. This condition called for me to fight to exercise courage in order to overcome these fears.

Gradually, I was able to develop the courage I needed just to maintain some sense of normalcy in my life and enjoy some aspects of my life with quadriplegia. Over several years, I found myself defeated by this anxiety of social interactions. I can only attribute the conquest of this fear and others alike, to intense prayer from within and from others.

This courage also factored into my decision-making. In particular, regarding the decision on whether or not to have the bullet that had been lodged inside my spine for approximately nine months removed.

Previously, none of my physicians would go near that bullet. They believed that it would be too dangerous to attempt to remove the bullet from the spinal cord, located so closely to the brain stem. Such a surgery would take extreme precision to be successful.

Also, the slightest error could cause severe brain damage, or even death.

Besides, I believe that the consensus opinion among and between most of my previous physicians was that the damage had already been done and removing it would not create a significant improvement in my condition, anyway. In their minds, the safest thing to do would be to just leave it.

But, my family and I had other ideas. We, as a unit, refused to accept this and resolved that it had to be removed. With this obstruction resting on my spinal cord, I had no chance of recovery. With the obstruction removed, at least I stood some chance at improving. Despite the tremendous danger involved, in order to reach the end goal I had in mind (a full recovery), I had to take that risk.

So, in my mind, it was settled. The next step, and just as difficult, was finding a surgeon who would do it.

My mother and I spoke with several neurosurgeons before we actually found our man. We visited Winston-Salem's Baptist hospital and spoke with the head neurologist there. The three of us had a lengthy discussion about the many intricacies involved in such a procedure after he reviewed the X-rays.

He explained that there was no guarantee that the procedure would help at all, but, stated that it was possible that the bullet could be pressing up against healthy nerve tissue causing extra bruising, which could cause some improvement, if removed.

He carefully explained the details of this procedure, and then, he shared with us the risks involved. The procedure would involve him having to remove vertebrae from my spine, and then very gently extracting the bullet itself, he explained.

Understandably, hearing him describe this difficult surgery aroused a great deal of concern among the two of us, especially when he stressed the fact that the surgery could possibly be fatal.

As we were deliberating over this difficult decision, my mother posed an interesting question. She asked the doctor, "if it were your son, would you do it?" Without any hesitation, he gave an emphatic "yes!" So, we agreed to proceed with the surgery, despite the possible dangers. When I reflect upon this conversation, it is evident to me, this question somehow "struck a nerve" in him. Perhaps he was a parent, himself, and could relate to the amount of concern my mother had at this time. Based on his response, I knew that this was a very confident surgeon and, more importantly, a man of tremendous faith.

It took knowing that for me to trust him with this complicated surgery. I certainly wouldn't want an unassertive, hesitant surgeon performing this procedure. Not on me!

On the day this surgery was to take place, my mother, brother, and I arrived at the hospital very early that morning. The operation was scheduled for approximately 8:00 a.m. that day in mid-July.

Upon our arrival, we were asked to sign consent forms. These forms were intended to release the hospital from any liability regarding further injury or death that could occur during this surgery. Signing these forms brought me face-to-face with this difficult reality; it is actually possible that I may not survive this operation. Needless to say, this certainly generated some concern on my behalf. However, I knew that my life, and outcome, was ultimately is God's hands and no amount of fear would keep me from proceeding with this surgery.

They rolled my bed into the waiting/recovery room where we waited for my number to be called. Just before the anesthesia countdown began, the three of us prayed for a healthy, successful operation. Shortly after that, I was transferred to the operating room where I almost immediately lost consciousness from the effects of the anesthesia. We definitely weren't off to a great start, but the essence of faith is belief and perseverance in the unseen.

I awoke several hours later to hear from the medical staff that the operation was a success. I was too groggy to express any type of emotion toward the staff, but I was tremendously grateful. Then, I was whisked away into my hospital room.

That night was basically a blur for me because most of the time was spent sleeping. This was fortunate because every single time I woke up, I was greeted by the most excruciating pain I had ever felt. I frequently yelled for the nurse to give me another shot of Demerol, to relieve the pain.

The next day I awoke, surprisingly alert and energetic, considering I had just undergone major spinal surgery less than 24 hours prior. I was so energetic that I immediately began to campaign to be discharged. I was scheduled to recover in the hospital for a week, but I was determined to exit as soon as possible.

After spending nearly six months in hospitals and rehab centers, I had grown completely weary of the hospital setting. For me, one more night in a hospital was much like a form of torture. I successfully negotiated my release and was discharged later that day.

My much anticipated arrival back at home came without much incident. The hospital staff—including my doctor—had warned me about leaving the hospital too early in my recovery stage. They warned that I could experience tremendous complications during the next couple of weeks. Fortunately, I didn't experience many side effects from the operation. I did, however, eagerly anticipate any changes in my situation, as a result.

For months, each day I intensely hoped to wake up and discover some kind of improvement. Two or three months had passed before I noticed any change at all. But, one night, while lying in bed staring at the television, I felt a strong sensation slowly traveling throughout my body. It felt like heat that generated in my back and then began to circulate throughout my limbs. I instantly attempted to move something—anything—on my body. Amazingly, I was able to raise my right arm and move my right foot, but just slightly.

I immediately began calling everyone I could think of to inform them of the good news. Relatively speaking, the movement was minute on the larger scale of things, but it was a small victory for me. I knew much more would be needed for me to even be able to stand—and ultimately, to walk. But, considering my state, previously, it was a giant triumph.

Before then, I was not able to feel anything, nor was I able to move a single muscle below my neck. Furthermore, all of my doctors had unanimously predicted that my condition wouldn't change for the remainder of my life. In fact, one physician—while in Baltimore—told my family upon their initial visit that, "the way you see him now, is the way he will remain for good." This change, however small it was, gave me a psychological edge that would sustain my optimism for years to come. I had already beaten their prognosis, and I was confident that I would continue to do so.

I was fueled by this "small" breakthrough, as well as the constant support of friends and family, and the prayers from multitudes of people throughout our region of the country. This was something that I was completely unaware of at the time. It is something that occurs mostly when we are unaware of it because of its intangible nature. But, deep down, I knew because of its result. It was the prayers of others that has always inspired and sustained me, even to this day.

This coming phase of my life was perfectly summarized by a Bible passage in which it states that, "*time and chance happen to everyone.*" In everyone's life there are moments of joy and pain. Oftentimes, these moments extend prolonged periods of time. Seasons of horrible storms engulf our lives just at the end of our brightest of days, it seems. Just ahead of me lay the most damaging of storms that I would ever experience, all over again.

As is common for many individuals who experience catastrophic injury or illness, especially ones that leave them non-ambulatory, the world seemingly moves on without them. For a moment, the world around me seemed to have stopped to rally to my aid. Now, times were changing, and the previous noticeable signs of support begin to diminish, and the number of visitations rapidly decreased. On top of that, a strong feeling of redundancy and impatience, resulting from a lengthy rehab routine without much sign of improvement, caused me to slip into a deep, dark depression for most of the next three years. Questions concerning my state of mind and state of being plagued me during every waking moment. Why me? What's next? When will I get better? As hard as I searched, I was never able to find the answers.

CHAPTER 6: WHAT NOW? Reality Shock

Nearly two years had passed by and I had already experienced a lifetime of changes. My life had been altered over and over again. Each joyful moment and accomplishment was soon met with yet another wave of disappointments. I had begun to come face-to-face with the reality of my circumstances.

The eagerly anticipated and much expected "miracle" had not occurred, and the actuality of such a breakthrough became more and more distant.

Depression was beginning to take hold of my life, severely depleting my optimism and damaging my self-esteem. I was beginning to believe all of the negative perceptions of my current condition and its outlook. I had begun to concede to the majority perception that I was forever destined to remain an "invalid" and only capable of maintaining a limited existence because of my injury. As a result, I slipped into a period of darkness where most of the dreams and aspirations that I always had for myself were no longer visible.

I had completely lost sight of any conceivable positive outcomes or purpose, and I began to focus on those things that were lost in my life. All of the plans of prosperity: in life, enterprise, family, school, etc. started to appear to be nothing more than wishful thinking. Anger and frustration took root in my heart, which caused me to question myself, my God, and probably anyone else who would listen. Why? I asked. Why?

"Everything is Lost!"

The harsh realities set in upon realization that things were more critical than I had previously believed. Sure, most of the medical personnel that I had come in contact with informed me of the critical nature of this condition. And I was constantly reminded of the gloomy prognosis: that I may never regain much functionality (physically or otherwise), walk again, or even worse, be able to live much longer.

Even though these phrases were constantly reverberating through my ears, since the early days following my injury, I never really accepted any of these ideas. I absolutely refused to believe it as such!

Some people might dismiss my attitude at the time as being merely a natural step in the process of dealing with tragedy—denial. But I never really believed that either.

Early in the game, I understood the significance and serious nature of my situation. However, I also understood well, the miraculous nature of my circumstances and the many, many miracles that had occurred in this journey, so far.

In fact, I was a miracle; so, surely God had much more in store for me than what I was hearing. It was that belief that had sustained me to this point, so when that began to fade, there wasn't much more to hold on to. I slowly began to see my circumstances for what they really were more than ever before. It was becoming blatantly obvious that my circumstances were extremely critical. I guess reality was finally setting in. Maybe I was reaching a point in time where I was becoming more willing and able to accept the fact that, no matter what happened from here, things would never be the same again, a horrifying revelation for anyone.

Relatively speaking, my health was in excellent condition. Even though I had this paralysis in my body, I had survived the initial stages of my injury without any lingering health problems. Physically, I was in great condition, much to the amazement of most of my physicians and caregivers. I attribute a lot of this to the excellent care I received at the hospitals that I lived in for six months following the shooting. But, I do believe that it was also an example of divine intervention and intention for me to be physically thriving despite the severity of my injuries.

Nevertheless, each day was a constant battle to maintain this physical status. My days began with a grueling workout; a physical therapy session that lasted for hours. Every evening ended with a similar routine, as well.

Simple tasks like bathing, eating, and getting dressed were performed with the complete assistance of another person, or persons. Day in and day out… that was my new reality. All of it was completely necessary, but becoming increasingly difficult for me to bear. The image of a previously vibrant, independent young man was shifting to one of a totally incapable "invalid," inside.

At night, I faced the impossible task of obtaining any sort of rest as I slept on a bed that rotated from side to side throughout the night, in order to prevent pressure sores from developing; just another concern, that if taken lightly could be devastating.

Besides that, each moment of each day was (and still is) spent with lingering aches and pains throughout my body. Involuntary muscle spasms frequently, without notice, sent my body into sometimes severe tremors. As a result, I required constant assistance and therapy in order to limit the potential negative effects. I was completely immobilized from a physical standpoint.

My transportation and travel merely consisted of an occasional trip to the doctor's office for a checkup. Sometimes,

I would go months without traveling beyond my front porch. This, too, became increasingly difficult for me to accept. All of these factors combined eroded away the belief and enthusiasm that until then had been so strong in me.

Depression is a hard disease to understand because it shows up in phases and slowly surrounds its victim. The dark cloud that accompanies it somehow obstructs your vision and makes things appear hopeless. That is how I began to feel—hopeless.

During this same time, I started to see a decline in the amount of visitors that I saw.

Throughout my entire life, I had always had many friends and loving family members around me. It was always something that I placed a tremendous amount of value on. So, when I experienced the tremendously generous initial response of support from friends and family, my belief in this form of sharing, and its importance, was only strengthened.

Not only that, for the first time I realized that I needed it, and that it was critical for my success in life. Therefore, as the wave of noticeable signs of support began to decrease, so did my mental outlook. The phone calls decreased and several of the individuals who were instrumental in my life at the time this shooting occurred, seemed to disappear.

My close friend and roommate, whom I roomed with for nearly two years at college, seemed to be one of them. He and I had grown to become very close since we first arrived on campus together. Up until this point, we were always the best of friends, but now I saw very little of him.

Even when we were together, I always felt that something was different; something between us—other than the obvious—had changed.

Our previously long, entertaining and in-depth conversations became short and distant. It was obvious that my injury made him uncomfortable and was having a tremendously harmful effect on our friendship. This was the case with several other friends of mine during this time. During most of my visits, I could actually see pain in the eyes of my other friends as well. It pained them to see me in my condition, bound to a wheelchair. And many of them often expressed to me how difficult a sight it was to see and how difficult the emotions were to bear. Ironically, I understood.

As for my former roommate, I could understand the difficulty he had faced during this course of events. To actually witness a close friend gunned down three feet in front of you had to be a damaging sight. Furthermore, the image of your completely healthy housemate or comrade, now restricted to travel with the aid of a powered wheelchair and breathing with the assistance of a machine strapped to its rear, had to be somewhat disturbing.

We were once the best of friends, with so much in common. As freshman college students, we immediately connected. We decided to room together and did so for the next year and a half. In fact, the two of us along with another classmate, Sed, developed strong bonds throughout our adventures (and misadventures) at the university. But immediately after the shooting incident, our bonds began to weaken, and now our associations progressed toward an immediate halt.

Unfortunately, this is a common scenario surrounding the lives of many who have experienced catastrophic events similar to mine. Relationships are often strained, damaged, and sometimes, lost because it is a difficult situation for everyone involved.

Having to witness a loved one suffer, at any point in time, is difficult. And that was the case for my college buddies, as well as the many other friends and acquaintances who seemed to be distancing themselves from me.

For a while, my life had frozen in time during my recovery and journey back toward the life I once knew. It seemed as though time had literally stood still for me to come to grips with my new reality and to make the many difficult adjustments required. However, their lives had to proceed. Even though they shared the pain that I was experiencing and sympathized with me, they couldn't grieve forever.

The problem arises when the physically afflicted individual internalizes these events as intentional acts of disregard, and I was no different. To me, it appeared to be blatant form of abandonment, which caused me to continually hurl insults at many of these individuals. Instead of attempting to reach out to these individuals and break those barriers to our relationships, I responded by further isolating myself, by choosing to associate solely with the few that I felt were my "true friends."

I have come to realize that the response I chose to adopt was completely selfish and inconsiderate. I was not the only victim in this set of circumstances. But, everyone who cared about me was hurt, as well. I know that now. Also, I was just as responsible for the breakdown in those friendships. It was my responsibility, too, to initiate communication with those friends with whom I had lost contact.

As it stands, I haven't talked with any of my close friends from college—a couple of which were in the car with me on that tragic night. Even though I haven't seen or heard from them in years, I understand completely. I also believe that we will be able to rebuild our friendships in the future. Nonetheless, the effect of this syndrome on me was tremendous. The deterioration of the many friendships I had previous to the injury helped pave the way to an awfully difficult, depressing period of my life.

Isolation became my world. With the exception of a few close friends and family members, I truly believed that I had been completely abandoned by everyone. All of my relationships had diminished, or so I thought, and I began to pay more attention to the memory of my tragic circumstances. The harshness of my physical condition began to become increasingly apparent, whereas before, I successfully dismissed my condition as a mere temporary obstacle to my promising destiny. Now, the negative prognosis that was handed to me started to become believable. I was beginning to believe that because I was confined to a wheelchair, I could no longer live a meaningful life, that is, until I had completely recovered — if that was even a possibility.

Because of this thought pattern, I was convinced that my social, educational, and relational needs would have to wait for my medical breakthrough to occur. I felt that I couldn't continue my education, nor participate in anything socially or recreationally fulfilling; things that I had always placed value in. I couldn't spend time with friends, travel, vacation, or just spend a relaxing day at the park. All of these simplicities were lost with my ability to walk, leaving me in an isolated environment. Everyone seemed to be moving on and enjoying every aspect of their lives, while I was left behind to face this limited existence, alone.

There were a few ever-present faces around me, like my mother, brother, cousins Malik and Keith, and several others. But, at the end of the day, I was the one who had to face the circumstances I was in. No matter how much someone sympathized with me or attempted to comfort me, no one could possibly understand the amount of suffering that I was experiencing.

In fact, I actually believed that I was the only one who was suffering through this ordeal.

The rollercoaster of emotions was disheartening and almost unmanageable as I struggled between hope, despair, depression, bitterness, disappointment, optimism, loneliness, anger, and frustration. The range of things that I felt represented the entire spectrum, and some days I never knew what was coming next.

Not only that, but I was beginning to feel ashamed of my physical appearance. As is common for many individuals confined to a wheelchair or afflicted by some physical disability, I was beginning to become overwhelmed by social anxiety. The looks and stares coming from individuals in the public—many of which were looks of concern and admiration for my strength and perseverance—were interpreted by me as abusive and insulting.

There I was, frightened of any sort of public appearances and even everyday face-to-face interactions because of my physical appearances; whereas, prior to my injury, I was the total opposite.

So, this was a totally new challenge for me. In a very short period of time, my entire perspective on life had turned upside down. Before, I was on top of my world and was convinced that nothing could knock me off of this "pedestal," and absolutely no goal was beyond my reach. Now, everything was beginning to seem unreachable.

As the days passed, I felt totally disconnected from everyone around me. There, isolated from the rest of the world, I would often present God with this very poignant question... why me?

To me, it seemed like the natural thing to do, to ask Him this. I never really expected Him to appear before me and reveal the reasons for, nor the terms of, my "punishment."

Yet, I did this every night from the early moments of my new life; an agonizing search that persisted for years with little result. In fact, I lost countless hours of sleep while expressing my anger, sadness, and disapproval with the omnipotent God.

I would think of dozens of others whom I felt were more deserving of this fate than I. "OK God," I would say, " I have done everything that I was supposed to do, so why haven't you healed me yet," I pleaded. Sure, I "walked" and talked faith, perpetually. I named it, claimed it, and even believed (somewhat) that my healing was close. I spent countless hours reading and listening to scripture related to my health. Maybe, I even believe that if I worked hard enough at these things and prayed rigorously enough, then God would reward me with healing.

Week after week, year after year, and yet, there was no change. I searched the Bible, and other related books, for the correct button to push that would change everything. I went through all of the motions, but nothing happened. Or at least not the thing that I wanted to happen. Before, I felt the abandonment from friends, family, and such. Now, I felt abandoned by my source and hope, a devastating feeling, indeed.

All of these dynamics contributed to a now more obvious, realization; I wasn't becoming depressed, I was depressed.

Until this phase of my life, I had coped fairly well with this ordeal. Emotionally, I immediately bounced back from the tragedy and its gloomy forecast. I mean, I was able to maintain a positive attitude throughout a very difficult hospital stint. My faith allowed me to maintain a healthy (somewhat reckless, according to some people) outlook. But then, my outlook didn't appear quite so optimistic as major depression began to take root in my life.

The broken friendships, loneliness, confusion, and certainly my physical condition, all factored into the deepening state of depression.

This state that haunted me was not your typical, situational depression that most of us encounter almost day-to-day. This depressive state totally consumed and immobilized me, interfering with all aspects of my life: eating, sleeping, social interactions, and overall drive. It certainly didn't help matters that during this time period I, like most men, mistakenly repressed most of these emotions, constantly attempting to persuade myself and others around me that I was OK. I feared that this would only reveal a dimple in my armor. To me, it was a sign of weakness, and I certainly couldn't allow that! Yes, it's a distorted viewpoint that causes so many of us to miss the very thing I was after, healing.

I was becoming increasingly angry because of my circumstances and often lashed out at those closest to me, as a result. I resigned myself to the fact that I could no longer enjoy once pleasurable activities: movies, sports, outings, and such. It was just me and my circumstances in this ongoing war of attrition, and they were certainly winning in this particular battle.

Why Me?

Over time I had been led to believe that the reason this tragedy occurred to me, and to others alike, was because of some hidden mistake somewhere in the past. I was, in a sense, tricked into believing this tragic event which occurred in my life was somehow my fault. What I was now experiencing was the result of some sort of karma-based reaction of some past behavior.

Unfortunately, too many afflicted individuals are haunted by this idea; that somehow each and every misfortune that occurs was a direct result of their past mistakes. These individuals live in a continual state of self-condemnation, unfortunately. And I, during this period of time, became one of those people.

Sadly, this mentality leaves so many of us lost in an endless search for answers in a realm where there are none. We constantly blame ourselves and condemn ourselves for misfortunes that have come our way; of which we have little or no control over. As did I... but yet the question still haunted my mind... why me? This agonizing, often unproductive inquiry plagued my life for much of this time. This is a question that plagues the minds of many of the afflicted. It is an age-old question; pondered over by countless numbers of people for no doubt, countless number of years.

Furthermore, there was the eternal question of, "why do bad things happen to good people." This is another common inquiry that generally surfaces in the face of tragedy.

Seemingly, the most undeserving and genuinely likable people seem to struggle with the most difficult of circumstances. Whereas others on the opposite end of the spectrum, who appear to lead less desirable lifestyles and even display more of an ill-will attitude towards others, seemingly live more prosperous lives.

This perceived syndrome appears to be all too common in our world, today. It is a confusing scenario that can leave the most well-intentioned individuals discouraged and upset at the perplexing and often sad state of affairs.

For me, it was extremely difficult to accept. Despite my own shortcomings and mistake-filled past of youthful indiscretions, I truly believed that I, for the most part, was a good person. I lived a principal-centered life in which I mainly placed the well-being of others above my own. So, why would God allow such a horrible tragedy to occur in my life?

Was it merely a result of bad "luck" or was there some divine purpose behind this tragedy? Was there an ultimate lesson for me to learn? Or, was there a spiritual combination code waiting to be discovered, or a certain button that had yet to be pushed, in order for God to respond? Also, why would He allow those individuals who were responsible, to get away with it? These questions would perpetually go unanswered causing me a tremendous amount of agony and nearly destroying my faith.

Thankfully, after years of torturing myself in such a way, I came to the realization that I was really only making things worse for myself. Not only was I wasting valuable time while precious moments were rapidly passing me by during this fruitless pursuit, but the depression and sadness that I was experiencing only mounted. As a result, the little amount of confidence and optimism that remained only continued to diminish, day by day; followed by my total self-identity. The cloud of depression was making me forget who I was and lose myself in its wake.

For years, prior to my injury, I had always been a person of confidence, ambition, and one who possessed a tremendous amount of drive.

Undoubtedly, this was a gift given to me from above. Even as a young teen, my mind was almost always geared toward future plans, as I would constantly dream up entrepreneurial schemes and plans, hoping for some key to achieving success in my life. But, I must admit, my behavior didn't always coincide with the accomplishment of these goals, but my attitude, overall, was firmly set.

In school, when challenged or told that I couldn't accomplish something, I usually responded to these challenges with tremendous fervor to prove myself. I jumped at every single entrepreneurial "opportunity," it seems, some of which cost me valuable time. On the other hand, all of these experiences served as training ground for me. But firmly entrenched in my psyche was the strong belief that sooner or later, I would hit the bull's-eye of success if I only continued shooting.

Now, the plans that I had laid for myself were completely rearranged, and for the first time since the injury occurred, I was beginning to lose sight of the ambition and drive I once possessed and no longer felt like shooting for anything. I had forgotten who I was (better yet, who God created me to be), as well as, His promises for my life. The reality of my condition and its bleak prognosis began to become believable and thus, too overwhelming for me to handle. Years had passed by without much sign of physical improvement. The resulting strain had deeply weakened my resolve and self-confidence. My identity was beginning to become rooted in, and defined by, my circumstances. I was conforming to the idea that I was destined to remain in a wheelchair, and my future would forever be limited because of my condition.

I had forgotten who I was; the gifts and the talents I once possessed were long gone, along with my ability to walk. God, why me?

There are many unfortunate stereotypes surrounding individuals with physical disabilities. Labels such as handicapped, invalid, cripple, etc., are distributed and expressed far too often in our society. Not only that, but these labels are often terribly damaging to the mindset of those suffering from disabling injuries and diseases. Also, the perception of those around us changes as these labels circulate. People tend to view the physically disabled as individuals who are: limited, lacking, and confined in mostly every way. When these labels continue to persist over time, we begin to believe many of these and as a result, make confessions of the doubt and fear one believes.

As for me, I started to accept some of the labeling, and as a direct result, my goals in life appeared unachievable. Education, marriage, family, health, and success in general, for the first time in my life appeared to be unattainable—and were quickly becoming unimaginable. The unfair stigmas that are often associated with the physically disabled had become acceptable for me. I had started to identify with these limiting characteristics. My dreams and goals would have to be placed on hold, I thought. My condition would have to be reversed before my life could continue. So, I did just that. I put everything on hold.

Regardless of the circumstances that surround us, they should have no weight in determining who we are; divine creations made by the Divine Creator! We may not be as pretty or handsome as others, we may have to deal with certain physical limitations and emotional or psychological challenges; truth is, most people we encounter believe that they are not quite "attractive" enough and are lacking and don't quite "measure up." We all are flawed according to most standards, but it is important for us not to allow these "flaws," temporal or otherwise, to define who we are inside.

My mistake was that I allowed my physical condition to totally confuse my identity. The Bible teaches us *"as a man thinks in his heart, so is he."* It was a concept that I stood upon for most of my life, often unknowingly. It was the very principal that, in my mind, allowed me to survive the terrible circumstances I had recently experienced during my fight for survival, and permitted me to do so with my optimism, intact. I believe that this passage embodies the mind of God, towards us. He wants for us nothing less than a productive, effective, and prosperous life; one that displays realized potential, rather than the opposite.

He views each of us, regardless of our environment or physical condition, as fully CAPABLE individuals. More exciting than that, is that He has fully equipped each of us with all that we need to fulfill our individual purpose. Despite what people may say about our potential, or lack thereof, our identity should always be aligned with God's perspective. Somehow I lost sight of that. And unfortunately for me, it cost me years of my life attempting to recapture it.

During this extended, agonizing search for answers, I inadvertently realized a deeper understanding of who our God was. Maybe that was part of the process. I wanted to know, why? *Why did this happen to me, and not someone else? Why won't you do anything about it?* For years, I was completely frustrated, and at times, devastated, at what I perceived as God's unwillingness to answer my queries. The effect of this exhausting search was this: I was presented with an ultimatum; give up on God, life, and my destiny because of my delayed response or continue to stand in the midst of trouble and seek God more diligently.

Because the change that I was hoping for did not happen when I expected it, I was often tempted to "throw in the towel." However, I stubbornly continued to seek him versus the alternative, resulting in a deeper relationship with Him. What I thought was an angered separation from the Father was actually just the opposite. His will was in operation the entire time. What he wanted from me was the relationship. Surely before, I had never read, studied, prayed, cried out, or needed Him so much in my life.

Sure, he could have restored my health in a moment's time, but He didn't. Why? I don't completely know. Maybe because I would have pushed Him aside again when I didn't need Him as much. Why did it happen to begin with? Who knows? Maybe, it was a case of a person being in the wrong place, at the wrong time? Maybe if it didn't happen that way, I may have completely forgotten about what He had done to bring me this far. But I do know that my relationship with

God was developed throughout this ordeal. Rather than changing my circumstances, He changed the way I viewed my circumstances. I began to view my challenges and so-called limitations as opportunities to utilize my God-given abilities (that He has already blessed each of us with) to persevere and triumph over them all. An amazing paradigm shift had occurred in my life, and I began to seek out opportunities to exhibit God's grace and mercy, instead of passively waiting for things to just happen. Time was certainly moving on, with or without me. Now, I had decided that it wouldn't be without me.

CHAPTER 7: MOVING ON

Clearing My Path

There comes a point in most of our lives, specifically, those of us who have experienced tragedy of some sort, where we finally get "fed up" with the circumstances. Sound familiar? Many of us can identify a time in our lives where the relentless call to change has overwhelmed our consciousness. No matter what the form of disappointment that has appeared in our lives, or how it appears, this sort of beckoning is impossible to ignore. This beckoning, I have come to know as destiny.

Destiny was desperately knocking in fear that he may be overlooked or unfulfilled; just because of the misfortunes that had surrounded me. Destiny was calling for me to take responsibility for my life, abandon that seemingly never-ending state of self-pity, and move forward with my future, in spite of. I had unconsciously cast away all confidence in myself and in God, my source. I chose to focus on what was missing from my life and what had been "lost," constantly blaming my physical condition for my lack of progress. I had concentrated on all of the negatives in my life and consequently, that's exactly what was manifesting before me. I had lost all sense of my own abilities because I was so focused on my disabilities and deficiencies. More importantly, I also had forgotten my identity, in God's eyes.

The previous five years or so had presented me with many twists and turns, ups and downs—mostly downs. The physical changes I had experienced and the many difficulties involved, along with the psychological turmoil that resulted; they all pushed my resolve to the very limits, and beyond.

Pain had stretched me beyond my own means and into a discovery of divine grace.

Strengthened by the prayer and support of many caring individuals, I managed to press my way through the trials that seemed to be ever-present. Now, I had emerged from a prolonged depressive state to an awakening of inspired living, motivated to seek challenges that before seemed impossible.

Before, I had grown complacent and accepted the idea that I would always be limited and would never fulfill the potential time once possessed. Now, I was intent on pursuing the dreams that were once so vivid to me, but had more recently become invisible.

However, there was one critical issue that needed to be resolved before I could progress in my journey to recovery, physically and emotionally. The issue that so urgently needed to be addressed was the issue of forgiveness, or the lack thereof. I was completely unaware of the fact that, for the number of years since my injury occurred, I had been harboring bitterness toward the individuals who committed this act. This may sound absolutely absurd to some, but those individuals that drove up beside us on that lonely highway, aimed a gun at me, pulled the trigger, and nearly ended my life; they had to be forgiven.

First, by harboring such bitterness in my heart for such an extended period of time, I had been kept emotionally bound. I was holding on to past circumstances that I, quite frankly, could do nothing about. I had never met or seen these people before. I had no clue of their whereabouts, whatsoever. The only visual I gathered during the time of the attack was a brief glimpse of three silhouettes as we passed by. At that point, there was nothing I could do to assist in their capture or incarceration.

What had happened to me on that night of October 13, 1995, could never be "unhappened" no matter how hard I prayed or how much I hoped that maybe it was just a horrible dream. There was nothing I could do about what had already happened. For the first time, I was realizing that this was a situation that I would have to confront rather than ignore. And I would have to release it rather than harbor it. Ultimately, I would have to forgive.

Now, I never really accepted my condition as fate and I always believed (and still believe) that it is a temporary one. But I had no chance of achieving true peace in my life because a high majority of my days were filled with anger toward the responsible party. At times I found myself completely unable to enjoy special moments with friends and family because I was so focused on harboring the anger and nursing my resentment. Even normally festive holidays became solemn to me because I was unable to release this anger. In effect, I was only hurting myself. Practicing forgiveness meant putting to rest the pain of the past. In order for me to be able to move on with my life, I had to come to grips with this dead issue.

Also, as a Christian I knew that it was my duty to forgive regardless of the intensity of the violation. Forgiveness is a basic tenet, a founding principle of salvation, in Christianity. Not forgiving would make me a hypocrite. In fact, regardless of religious affiliation or identification, the truth remains that harboring bitterness and unforgiveness is not only counterproductive, but it is an actively self-destructive force. The unforgiveness and bitterness that I was refusing to let go of was slowly destroying me. It was limiting my ability to enjoy moments with friends and family, and in fact, I found it difficult to find any kind of enjoyment or optimism in my life at all. Through my unforgiveness, I had allowed the perpetrators of this wretched crime to victimize me twice. For me, this anger was completely immobilizing, preventing me from maintaining any effectiveness in my life and blocking any blessing that I had hoped to attract in my life (peace, success, healing, etc.); none of the things could ever be attained if I were to continue holding on to this sort of negativity in my life.

The exact moment in time where I came to this realization is completely vivid in my memory, even today. One night, while lying in my dark room angrily cursing these individuals that I have never seen before, I realized just how destructive and even, ludicrous it was for me to continue with this attitude. It didn't come in the form of some speech, sermon, or from some sort of positive attitude-based literature, but it came in the form of a quiet, still awakening inside of me that no doubt came from above. Immediately, I knew exactly what I needed to do to stop this anguish. I said aloud, "I forgive the individuals who have injured me, and I pray that the grace of God presides over their lives." That very moment represented a profound moment of release. Much of the anguish and frustration that had been collecting inside of me was, at that moment, beginning to disappear.

I, myself, am not capable of such a feat. But, I managed to do so only with His divine assistance. I, today, continually pray for these individuals. It is often difficult to keep those negative attitudes buried, but, I truly believe that if I saw the perpetrators today, nothing but good words would come from my mouth. It certainly was a struggle for me to reach that point—that I could make this claim. But honestly, no amount of bitterness, worry, or complaining would ever generate any change, or at least not the changes I desired. I didn't really know what to expect in my future, but this ordeal taught me one valuable lesson. The shooting incident itself would not keep me from moving on with my life, but, harboring bitterness because of an unforgiving heart, would.

This period of my life culminated with some profound revelations regarding my personal outlook and attitude. I had experienced a tremendous amount of pain and disappointment, during what I like to refer to as the "dark ages" of my recovery. But the end result was a rediscovery of who I was and just as importantly, what I was capable of.

I don't know exactly what triggered the change in attitude or the epiphany I experienced, but it succeeded in bringing about a much-needed change in my attitude and in my life.

Specifically, I began to shift toward an eagerness to achieve, in spite of my circumstances. Time and frustration had taken their toll on me, and I was ready for a change to happen. Five or so years had passed, and I was no closer to my goals in life than I was before this set of events, I realized. Furthermore, I discovered that time would proceed with or without me. I had become frustrated with my life, during that time.

Throughout the duration of my recovery to that point, I had been constantly told how strong I was and fortunate I was to have survived the shooting. Friends and strangers alike, constantly expressed their admiration for my resiliency and the fact that I was able to smile (even though it was often an artificial smile), in lieu of my circumstances. "I can't believe it, you seem so content," they would say.

That was exactly the problem. I had grown content with my circumstances and accepted them as fate. I had convinced myself that I was just "waiting on God." And the same time, it is my belief, that He was waiting on me; to use what He had given me already to generate change. Once I realized this fact, it angered me, completely. The end result was that my old dreams and desires, which were seemingly lost, were beginning to become visible again. My focus had now shifted to finding a sort of independence in different areas of my life, and my desires were now to thrive, not just survive.

Instead of "why," the new question became, "where do I start?" I knew something needed to be done and I sort of believed that, what ever it was, I could do it. Several years ago I had set myself on the course of achieving the goal of obtaining my college degree. I often strayed off of the course, though, while placing more importance on my social life and partying experiences. But, for the years following my injury I was convinced that this particular goal was no longer attainable.

I again found value in my own education and I had set my sites on attending school again. I realized that many great individuals in the past have gone on to do great things in life, with little or limited education. So, I don't believe that education is the only key to an effective life. In other words, a certain level of education or a specific degree has never guaranteed a successful, fulfilling life, to anyone. In fact, many of our most important educational experiences come from everyday life, instead of colleges or universities. But for me, this goal quickly became an overwhelming passion.

I soon visited a local university with the intent to explore my options. I approached the staff at the university about continuing my education. As I dug deeper, I discovered that it was very much possible and much easier than I ever thought. Something that I, for years believed would be a difficult, lengthy process, turned out to be somewhat, trouble-free.

Thanks to the tremendous support and care I received from the disability services department (a department designed specifically for the purposes of assisting individuals like myself with their educational pursuits, including counseling, motivation, accessibility issues, etc.), I began to realize the actuality of attending classes again, with thousands of others.

Admittedly, I wasn't necessarily enthused about being in the public view again; in fact, I was somewhat fearful and attempted to "back out" several times. But the staff, who have since become great friends, gave me the encouragement that I needed. So, despite the fears and concerns, I continued along with the process and made the necessary arrangements to reattempt the college "experience" during the summer of 2001.

My first day approached rather quickly that summer. And for many days leading into this journey, I felt a tremendous sense of anxiety. The feeling was similar to that of a freshman stepping on to a college campus for the very first time; my first day resuming my college pursuits. On top of that, my first course was a public speaking class, no less. So, I would immediately have to face those fears of public situations. In fact, one of our very first activities was to get in front of the entire class and introduce ourselves and give a brief synopsis of our individual backgrounds. Needless to say, mine generated significant interest throughout the group.

The response I received from the class on this first day and throughout the semesters was completely different from what I had envisioned. Instead of the students withdrawing from me and distancing themselves, like I had expected, they did just the opposite. There was a genuine concern for my well-being, as well as a strong interest in my example of survival and overcoming. Everyone was generous and supportive.

The most surprising thing was that they seemed to draw strength and encouragement, themselves, merely from my presence there in the classroom.

I was obviously conspicuous (wheelchair and respirator in tact), but my attendance alone was becoming an inspiration for the others, it seemed. I quickly befriended several interesting people in the classroom and throughout the entire university as well. My first experience since resuming my education helped me to realize that I actually possessed a crucial message and an important voice, and that people wanted to hear it.

It was in my speech class that a message was beginning to be formed inside of me and being developed in anticipation of its delivery. My professor was awfully supportive and nurturing to my needs, but she didn't cut me any slack either. She had the same expectations and placed equal requirements on me as with each of her students. It was just the vote of confidence that I needed. For the first time since my injury occurred, I was beginning to recognize a sense of purpose in my everyday life.

The next few years of my life served as an awakening period. I was beginning to experience an abundance of pleasurable times all over again. As crazy as it may sound, I began to take pleasure in joining a classroom full of students and even burying myself in a pile of textbooks. These are simple things, these sorts of simple pleasures, I quickly realized had been unjustifiably vanished from my life. And for a long time it seemed to be impossible to regain my sense of being.

Though it was an awfully minute step in the grand scale of things, it represented a tremendous stride in my recovery and reestablishment into a life of independence. Although I couldn't write or turn pages and such—which made this task increasingly difficult—I was completely grateful for this opportunity and I accepted this new challenge with a newfound level of expectation and complete enthusiasm.

I was completely reliant upon the assistance of others or adaptive technology to perform any of these otherwise simple, tasks. But each and every step toward the goal of "normalcy" presented challenges that were new and different than anything I had faced previously, but a more dominating force, my desire for independence and self-sufficiency, overshadowed any fear that was in me. So, I gradually continued on that path. The more I progressed, the more I realized that there was never really any physical condition that was limiting me… it was me.

After many years of restraining me from maintaining any semblance of an effective life, a strong desire to generate independence in all areas of my life had arisen. My ultimate desire, again, was to fully recover from my injuries and stand, walk, run again. My faith can always be in God to bring this to fruition. But after many years of anticipation and the resulting disappointment, I realized that until this dream materialized, I would have to be productive and not allow my life to evaporate into thin air. Besides, the more I excused my lack of productivity to my physical condition, the more I became depressed.

Finally, I allowed myself to begin creating a new reality for myself. Our God, who is the essence of creativity has instilled in each and every one of us the ability to create, produce, craft, and build. We were designed to create, so I began to construct a new version of myself.

Though it wasn't completely obvious to me as to what exactly was going on inside of me, I knew that there was some divine force overshadowing my own abilities and confidence, pushing me along. Once I made this leap of faith and resumed my education, attempted to live independently and become self-sufficient in my many areas of my life, and accepted responsibility for my activity, or lack thereof, I began to recognize the development that was taking place.

Again, the steps can be viewed as "baby steps" to some, things that may appear as minute, normal progression in the life of a young adult, but to me, it was a considerable victory. Society had labeled me incompetent and powerless, simply because of my physical condition. Tragically, I had believed it for several years. But, no longer would my circumstances, or other people's opinions of my circumstances, govern me.

The next, and probably the most critical step toward my development of an effective, purposeful life, was a direct gravitation toward interdependence in all areas of my life. For so long I had been totally reliant and dependent upon others for each and every one of my needs. The dependence still exists to an extent because many of my physical disabilities still persist to this day. But the dependence that was so harmful to me at the time, and to many other completely healthy individuals, was the psychological dependency that existed. Psychological dependency like: allowing negative people's perceptions to rule my actions, or the dependency on a life that was completely stress free because of the decreased pressure surrounding a mindset with little expectation or vision.

Independence then resurfaced in the form of a renewed commitment to continuing my education and other pursuits of self-actualization. Now, a more compelling desire had taken over, and that was the desire to progress into an existence where I would begin to see purpose manifest.

Independence was certainly a giant leap from where I was just a few years previous and is certainly praiseworthy for any individual stifled by any form of oppression—spiritual, emotional, physical, or otherwise. But there came a point in my life where I felt completely unfulfilled and separated from what I was created to do; who I was created to be.

By nature we are social individuals and require constant fellowship with others just to maintain any sanity, whatsoever. Even members of the plant world and animal kingdom require constant contact and communication to survive. As much as we deny it, we all need associations and healthy relationships with others to endure. And I discovered that the same was true for me. When we deprive ourselves of this most basic need, we often open the door for depression, defeat, and despair to set in. We need to edify and to be edified, despite our level of confidence and self-image. We definitely need each other to survive, in every sense.

So, with that being said, I gradually proceeded to "spread my wings" further and purposely seek out opportunities to establish relationships with others. No longer fearful of all social situations, I intently sought opportunities to converse with complete and total strangers and share myself, my story, etc., hoping that it would benefit someone else, and absolutely certain that it would benefit me. I attempted to repair and recover so many of the associations and friendships which had been lost for so long. I never really believed that I was destined to remain in that isolated, lonely state for much longer.

My focus began to shift in the direction of becoming an effective individual, despite my physical limitations. The kind of effectiveness that I am speaking of has nothing to do with activity or productivity, for that matter. Since the injury, I had always maintained a degree of mental stimulation through reading, educational programs, the Internet, and so on. I even maintained a healthy amount of physical activity, as well.

Though I was productive, in many respects, I wasn't very effective (or as effective as I was called to be). This type of effectiveness is not universal, as it is completely unique to the individual, himself. Effectiveness stems from a specific and direct "calling" and it is completely unique to that individual person. A person's degree of effectiveness is not determined by anyone else but God Himself, and it is not influenced by the external factors like: physical condition, status, titles, economic status, or any environmental factors. That individual may be totally effective and purposeful, totally absent from immediate recognition, accolades, or many other trophies that we use to label an effective individual. In fact, one can be completely effective and influential from a sick bed in a hospital's intensive care unit. Consider the lives of our historic figures and the lessons their lives have exhibited. We all know the testimony of Helen Keller... and the impact she made in American history in spite of her so-called limitations and disabilities. We are all called to effect change in our environment. It requires us to relinquish our self-centeredness and seek to fulfill the needs of others around us. I believe this attitude epitomizes the mindset of an effective individual. And somewhere along the line, I recognized that I had that exact same responsibility.

A very pivotal moment in my development as a person of effectiveness occurred during a "chance" meeting with an individual who would turn out to become a very influential person in my life.

During a curious moment I had decided to visit a local church, one that I had heard many positive comments about. Since committing myself to a life in service to God, I had come in contact with many church leaders and members in my area which I have had the pleasure of developing special relationships with. But, at this particular service that my girlfriend and I attended, I felt an overwhelming sense of familiarity and comfort. There was a climate of peace that circulated throughout the room that undoubtedly emanated from the leadership, speaking from the platform that night. It was a very powerful experience that led me to return the following week in order to meet with the pastor of that church. I am not quite sure why I made this particular appointment, other than, to introduce myself and to express my appreciation for the wonderful service I had experienced. However, the meeting turned out to be much more than that.

After exchanging pleasantries and introductions the conversation shifted to more of an emotion-filled confessional. Somewhere in our conversation I felt totally compelled to share the details surrounding the shooting incident that had crippled me for around seven years, at that point in time. I totally spilled my guts, so to speak, and didn't leave out one single detail. I gave a complete timeline of events that took place on that Friday night on October 13, 1995. I explained my thoughts, actions, prayers, etc. on that night. I also described many examples of God's supernatural intervention for me on that night, and so many nights, thereafter.

Even though I didn't approach this meeting with any intentions of venting in such a way, he somehow, managed to pull it out of me. This individual, Bishop George W. Brooks, has come to be a tremendous influence in my life and a wonderful mentor, as well.

But, shortly after this lengthy monologue, he immediately stressed to me how incredibly moving my story was and just how important it was for others to hear it. And I agreed. He recognized the potential impact that this testimony could have on the lives of many, which served as a confirmation of a belief, or even more so, a vision that had been brewing inside of me ever since the injury occurred. He believed so strongly in my story's potential impact that he presented me with the opportunity to share my experiences with his congregation (no doubt, more than 4,000 people) that Sunday morning, only two days away.

Now, I wasn't exactly thrilled at this proposition being that the full extent of my public speaking experience only consisted of a few presentations in speech class at the local university. So, I was understandably intimidated by this proposition. Nevertheless, we came to an agreement that I would do so, but with a week to prepare.

That appointed day approached rather quickly for me. It seemed as if that week was the shortest week in my life. I got very little rest that week because of the overwhelming anxiety that had built up with each day. But, I managed to muster the encouragement to perform this task. This resolve must have come, in part, from an understanding there was the potential that sharing my experiences with these people could have a tremendous impact on a few lives. Even more compelling was the strong sense of responsibility I possessed. I felt responsible to myself, to everyone who extended love and support to me throughout this ordeal, and to God, Himself, as a symbol of appreciation for this miracle of life, which had been preserved.

With these things in mind, I continued on with this message; strengthened by His empowerment, I was able to fight back the overwhelming intimidation and fear that I faced.

Surprisingly, the speech ended with a resounding applause from the massive crowd, which definitely generated a feeling of success and fulfillment of a very critical step in my life. An even more telling sign of the success of this message, more important than any applause, was the droves of young men and women who approached the altar for prayer, following the speech. That was the moment of epiphany for me!

Sure, I proved to myself and others that I could surpass certain expectations, or label-based limitations; but, I then realized that there was purpose in my life. Through all of my struggles and setbacks, I had now found renewed purpose in my life.

Fortunately, I have since then had many other opportunities to share my story with various churches, organizations, schools, etc. since that precious moment. I began to discover that there was indeed hope, power, and blessings within my story and that there are great numbers of people wanting and needing to hear it.

This period of time of my life was representative of an awfully critical stage of development. It was more important than the period of time wherein my injury occurred and the resulting experiences, thereafter. It was certainly more important than the period of years that I spent wallowing in depression and allowing those self-inflicted psychological restraints to persist and mentally cripple me.

Beginning with the release of bitterness that had been encased inside of me, the wheels of life began to turn, again. The same bitterness, whether directed at someone else or directed toward your present circumstances is a tremendously destructive force, as I have found.

My focus began to shift toward intended future rather than the disappointing, depressive present state that I was in, one that was only temporal. I found myself arriving into a state of independence where I was forced to assume responsibility for my circumstances and move on with those aspirations that were important to me, like: my education, relationships, self-sufficiency, vocation, life in general. I had begun to embrace life for the miracle that it is. More importantly, I began to identify my true purpose in this lifetime; what I was created to do.

My divine construction called for me to walk in the purpose that I was designed for, no matter what my circumstances looked like. I was created (as were many who may be reading this) to inspire, uplift, share, mobilize, and lead.

Contrary to many of the reports that were issued to me following my injury, my circumstances only developed my outlook on life and its challenges and enhanced my sense of purpose and meaning, rather than the opposite. It was an educational process also. It was an education into the appropriate responses and mentality that were necessary to adopt, when faced with adversity. Also, it was a growth process that I needed to endure in order to teach and encourage other people to do the same.

Set in motion was a process culminating with the discovery of my destiny. And I have come to realize that nothing can halt divine purpose once it is in motion, not even physical limitation.

CHAPTER 8: Responding to Adversity: Why Not Me?

How are we to respond to the inevitable appearance of adversity when it comes into our lives? I don't know if there is a single, definite answer to this question. Most of us incorporate what other resources we have available to us at the time. That's really all we can ask for; to make the most of our current position in life.

However, I have been fortunate enough to observe the lives of a number of individuals who have successfully confronted personal challenges, over and over again. This type of individual maintains an attitude that no level of pain, disappointment, or obstacle will outweigh their will to overcome. These individuals are tremendously inspirational to me. Their attitudes are so uplifting and testify to the ideal manner in which we should all approach our difficulties in life.

I have learned so much from observing this type of individual, and I can only pray that my life provides the same testament of how to respond when faced with adversity.

History provides us with countless examples of individuals who have persevered over seemingly insurmountable circumstances to accomplish great things. Most of these individuals possessed a certain element in their character that, in itself, provides a great deal of inspiration and can be tremendously inspirational for those of us who study their testimonies. One of those individuals whose story I have found to be very inspirational for me and provides an excellent example of how to face adversity is Victor Frankl and his triumph over severe challenges and adversity.

Viktor Frankl was a Holocaust survivor who withstood unspeakable horrors in various concentration camps, including Auschwitz, one of the most renowned camps in Nazi Germany. Frankl, in his autobiography, *Man's Ultimate Search for Meaning*, describes many of these terrors he and his fellow prisoners experienced. The experiences depicted in his story, describes some of the most grueling, agonizing events imaginable. He was facing a day-to-day struggle to maintain hope (for himself as well as others), an almost impossible goal considering the circumstances in which he faced, and understandably so. On a daily basis, he and other inmates would have to witness the lives of their comrades unjustifiably taken, knowing that at any moment they could follow. Over a number of years, Frankl and his brothers experienced this horrific genocide, and yet, he survived these difficult circumstances to later become one of the most prominent psychologists of the 20th century. He used his Holocaust experience as a discovery experience, as well as, a groundbreaking launch into his field of psychotherapy.

To me, the most fascinating aspect of his story is the discoveries into his (and others) ability to overcome the harshest of circumstances simply by making the decision to do so. Frankl described a scenario, while in prison, where many prisoners learned to be helpless. At one camp, he claimed that the guards would approach the prisoners, deliberately, and tell them they would never leave. According to Frankl, all of those who succumbed to this belief soon died. And those who didn't, including Frankl, survived. Professional exploits aside, I believe the most beneficial, encouraging aspects of Mr. Frankl's story are the attitudes that were adopted by he, and his fellow survivors. They adopted the belief that no matter what they experienced, no matter what they witnessed, they would persevere.

I realize that these circumstances describe one of the most horrible events in the history of our world, and my comparisons are by no means intended to make light of the experiences of those who were victimized. But, sharing this testimony provides a great deal of perspective on the psychology of survival and provides tremendous lessons for us all. We may probably never experience such personal tragedy, but we should all adapt similar responses to the tragedies that occur in our personal lives.

Again, his story describes the most extreme circumstances, but there is much to be gained from it, nonetheless. Such attitudes are admirable, and should be a goal for many of us (to reach such a level of faith and determination). But another, more contemporary story of triumph, and one that is much more personal for me, is the story of the life of Christopher Reeve. Like Frankl, Reeve's story provides a tremendous example of remarkable human character and drive. I am writing in light of his recent passing, so this story and personal recollections mean so much more to me now.

Christopher Reeve was an individual who experienced personal tragedy in the form of a horrible accident which left him completely paralyzed, at the pinnacle of his success. Prior to the accident, Reeve had enjoyed many years of success as an accomplished actor. Besides his acting career (which had been extremely prosperous), Reeve also enjoyed a prosperous family life. Seemingly, all of these things had been lost on the day that he was thrown from his horse and suffered a broken neck which led to his paralysis. Even more intriguing is how he responded to this "tragedy." Reeve not only continued to be a strong, effective family man, but continued his success in front of and behind the cameras, as he starred in and developed several other films. More importantly in my mind, were the many other exploits he performed for humanity's sake.

Chris succeeded in providing a statement for an entire sector of the world's population, that is, the physically disabled (or any one who has experienced the tragedy of loss, of any kind). This legacy was indeed an extraordinary one. Chris responded to his tragic circumstances in a way that generated optimism for countless numbers of individuals, worldwide. Prior to this unfortunate accident, most of the individuals facing this battle with paralysis had little voice or recognition in today's society. Meaning those who were afflicted by physical paralysis or any physical disability for that matter, often faced shame and embarrassment in many public settings. As often was the case, these individuals were shunned in many areas of society. The tremendous awareness he was able to generate greatly increased the amount of concern toward their needs and an appreciation for their individual plights.

His life provided a much-needed optimism to the lives of many people, particularly those experiencing spinal cord injuries. His example galvanized many individuals and organizations by showing that the realm of possibilities were unlimited, if an individual only believed. Here was a man who had "everything," according to how most of us define success. He had a prosperous career, family, and life in general. With his accident, and subsequent, injuries, many people believed that everything he had accomplished was lost. However,

Chris' life proved the complete opposite. Not only was he able to continue forward with all of his personal aspirations, but he also showed multitudes that they could too. Regardless of their degree of loss, form of tragedy, or severity of injury, his example encouraged others that success and achievement were still possibilities despite their circumstances. A remarkable legacy to strive for, indeed!

On top of that, he successfully generated an enthusiasm throughout the world of spinal cord research that never really existed beforehand (at least, not to the same extent).

Doctors, caregivers, patients, their families, and friends began to believe and become enthusiastic about the possibilities of restored health to themselves, their friends, relatives, or patients. Hope was established in the hearts of many, the previously hopeless. Through his efforts and voice, he provided reasons for individuals to carry on with their lives and the "business of living" in general, whereas many believed previously, that there was no reason for living, whatsoever. With a cure in sight, many received restored meaning and purpose in life. In effect, because of this reestablished faith and energy, there was a tremendous spillover effect into other aspects of many people's lives, where many began to believe in a world of other possibilities, as well.

Before, such things were unthinkable, but now they are obtainable. It is unfortunate that he was unable to see his dream materialize. Nevertheless, the impact he had on so many lives throughout the world will remain a powerful legacy that will never be forgotten.

Personally, the impact that he made on me will carry on for a very long time. During that very first encounter we had together in the hospital room at Kessler in West Orange, New Jersey, I was motivated to vigorously fight this battle with paralysis and to passionately pursue my individual purpose (though it may be somewhat different than his). "Besides, he has lost so much more than I," I thought, and he still remains optimistic. "Why can't I?" Just from the brief time that we spent together and my observance of his efforts, over the years since, I have learned a great deal from his example of selflessness. Hopefully, I will be able to incorporate the same characteristics in my life and ministry.

The previously mentioned testimonies provide tremendous examples for us to follow in our personal walk, regardless of our backgrounds, religion, or otherwise. They testify of the resiliency of the human character when faced with the most difficult of circumstances. It is stories like these that motivate and inspire the lives of millions. They are just a couple of the many stories that have provided me with encouragement to continue with my personal goals and my purpose in God. I, just like most of us, deal with the tremendous amount of setback and adversity, daily. Much of my challenge stems directly from this physical paralysis that I face. However, adversity doesn't discriminate; it will affect one and all, eventually. It may not appear to the extreme as previously depicted, but we all will experience some adversity in time, and none of it is necessarily welcomed. But, the adversity that you may experience in your day-to-day lives is just as important to you as my struggles are to me; none are more or less significant to the individual(s) involved.

If there is one lesson that I have learned (or am learning) through this challenging ordeal, it is how to respond to adversity when it comes.

We should respond by first changing our perspective toward that challenge in our lives. We must always retain our optimism. I know it seems basic, and no doubt easier to say than do, but it is a fundamental and obvious principle to apply although many difficulties in life cause us to forget about it.

There may be times when difficulties are so overwhelming that we may just throw up our hands and surrender. In times like these we are often tempted to completely abandon our optimism and give up hope for any form of turnaround. But I believe that optimism is a critical characteristic for us to have in our life's journeys. Not only that, I also believe that it is a gift in itself. A gift from above, granted to us all, in order to help us along the way. Many of us, however, often times decide not to accept and exercise this gift. It is not necessarily a given that individuals we encounter day-to-day, are generally optimistic to their life and its possibilities. In fact, I am beginning to recognize more and more that most people are just the opposite. This is probably a direct result of the constantly increasing troubles and stress that are common to all of us in everyday life. But, just as the individuals mentioned previously, we must choose to remain optimistic in the most difficult of circumstances. There is a common thread in the character of individuals who have accomplished great things and overcome tremendous obstacles — and that common thread is optimism.

No matter what the circumstances are or how grueling they may be, the first step toward any breakthrough must be BELIEF! We must understand that anything is possible with the essential ingredient of belief, but nothing is possible without it. We must believe in something—Someone—higher, greater, and more powerful than ourselves. Sure, it is a simple, fundamental concept; one that we hear about time and time again in all of the latest motivational seminars and materials. So much so, that these concepts have nearly become clichés, and their effects are rarely, sustainable (barely long enough for us to reach the next seminar). However, I believe that we must simply become habitual believers and exercise the gift of optimism in all aspects of our lives in order to overcome the obstacles that appear in all of our lives.

Why Not Me?

As an avid reader of quotes I often look to them for inspiration during times of difficulty. I believe it is important to study the lives of story figures who have lived through similar circumstances such as ours, or people whose life story was one of inspiration. Many of the quotes that they leave behind often provide tremendous insight into the challenges they faced and their strategies for overcoming, as well. There is one interesting quote that has always been a favorite of mine, and is the basis of this section:

You look at things the way they are and you say 'why,' I look at things that never were and I say, 'why not?'
-George Bernhard Shaw

This was a quote given to us by the individual who was fully accomplished, he was a playwright, author, essayist, you name it. In the world of accomplishment, he was extremely successful, well into his nineties. But this statement provides profound insight into the psychology of a believer, a believer whose lifestyle is one of belief, not just for a particular event to occur, but one who perpetually believes, and is not confined by any form of perceived limitation or impossibility. The kind of belief that I am speaking of is not just an activity or even a stance regarding a certain desired outcome. To me, it describes an unwavering faith that anything one desires in life is possible, without any exception.

The Bible illustrates such belief time and time again, in particular, one passage, *"I can do all things through Christ who strengthens me, (Phil.4: 13),"* illustrates this lifestyle perfectly, considering the locale and setting surrounding the writer, at the time. Here is what Jesus said about the certain likelihood of difficulty in our lives, and the appropriate response: *In this world you shall have tribulation, but be of good cheer because I have overcome the world.* This passage attests to the unavoidable troubles that will occur in each of our lives. It may vary in form or fashion, but regardless of its intensity, it is undoubtedly significant to that individual. It may not be in the form of a debilitating injury like mine, however it is no less significant. To me, what is most intriguing about this passage is the insight provided concerning our ability to take control, take responsibility for our responses. The Lord said, *"... be of good cheer..."* In other words, we have the innate ability and power to choose how we respond to adversity.

Adversity is not always a BAD thing! Oftentimes, adversity will bring out the best in people. There are countless examples of historic figures that have used their adversity as an opportunity to develop character and inner strength. For many, it has served as a clarion call to effect change in magnificent ways. The very same adversity that has been destructive for some, has been a mobilizing force for others. Some of their lives have been written about, like the individuals mentioned previously, but many of these testimonies have gone unnoticed. But, the common thread in the makeup of these individuals is their proactive response to their challenges. They didn't necessarily submit to adversity as a force that would automatically generate those damaging emotions, but viewed it as a mere obstacle in route to the fulfillment of their destiny.

If there's one piece of advice I can leave with you, it is to recognize life as a gift and not a given.

I have a close friend and relative with whom I often consult when my challenges seem to be a little overwhelming. Lee Rouson, an inspiring individual to say the least. He was a former NFL athlete who has now turned to the ministry, and has dedicated himself to evangelistic missions in countries throughout the world. I truly respect the vision and intensity he possesses, and that's why I often consult him when I feel down or depressed. Somehow he always manages to say something that lifts me up. I will often called Lee and ask, "What's going on?" And right on cue, he enthusiastically responds by saying, "I am just opening up this present, this gift that God has for me, each day!" The first time I heard this, I was truly amazed by the profoundness of this simple statement. Though it was short, it certainly ministered to me and spoke volumes about the necessary approach one should take to navigate through life. It is symbolic of an ideal, invigorating perspective on life and a true sense of what it means to live in the NOW. Every waking moment of our lives is truly like a gift—a present—to behold.

At a previous time in my life, following the shooting incident and subsequent injuries, I found myself mired in a pit of confusion and disarray. I spent several years of my life continually and intentionally lamenting the tragic circumstances I found myself in, and at the same time, passively waiting for some eventual change to occur in my health, and life in general. All the while, days, weeks, even years, of my life were slowly disappearing. We should value each of our present moments because that is really all that we have. The past is just that and no amount of worry could ever change its misfortunes. Likewise, tomorrow is not promised to anyone. We should make a considerable effort to value the present moment and all that it provides. There are relationships to build, successes to enjoy, opportunities to seize, lessons to be learned, now, and in this present moment.

If we choose to spend the present time lamenting the past or aspiring toward some future event we will miss out on the wonderful moments available for us right now. There is a common saying that says, "life is what happens to us while we are making future plans." While our focus is centered on some future event to occur, moments, time, life itself is slowly passing us by. I am not implying that goal setting is a worthless pursuit, but we should not fall so much in love with some future goal, status, promotion, etc. that we overlook the many miracles of our daily lives.

To successfully weather any challenge, it is necessary that we seek a higher power than our own when confronted with difficulties that may arise. During a time where we are surrounded by so many troubles, it is imperative that we continually incorporate the assistance that is available to us by our God. Much of the literature and teachings that flood our markets today are centered around such concepts as self-improvement and self-empowerment. They are relevant messages for today's world and are tremendously valuable.

However, I have come to realize that such ideas are rather incomplete. No matter how empowered we are as individuals or how motivated we become, we are still incomplete in our limited selves. We can't do it all by ourselves. We have inefficiencies by nature, and it is God's divine presence that completes us. For we are reminded that it is His grace that is sufficient for us during trying times.

We were created with unlimited potential, along with our flaws as well. In order to see our potential fulfilled and our purpose realized, we need Him! To assume that any of us are complete within ourselves is absolute folly. And to adopt this mentality would mean totally disconnecting ourselves from the source of our being—our Creator. In order to accomplish our goals, purposes, or achieve fulfillment, we must look to and rely upon a greater power than our own. We must continually look to the higher power that is God.

The Bible provides us with the ample reason to persevere in prayer and not surrender hope. The living words found therein have always sustained me. As I write, I am reminded of that poster that hung there on the wall of my hospital room:

They that wait upon the Lord, **shall** *renew their strength*
they shall mount up with wings as Eagles
they shall run and not grow weary
and walk and not faint.

This message served as a constant reminder that there was an unlimited source of strength available to me if I would just continually ask of and anticipate His help; then I would survive my troubling circumstances. I was in a position of forced reliance upon God for any chance of escape. Had I not been forced into this position, I may have just relied upon my own capacities which would have been insufficient and undoubtedly tragic. During a period of time where death was always lingering just around the corner, it was my affirmed admission, acceptance, and acknowledgement of God and his thoughts toward me that enabled me to persevere.

I know the thoughts that I think toward you, saith the Lord
plans to prosper you and not to harm you,
to give you a hope and a future (Jer. 29:11)

With such promises as this presented to us, nothing can destroy our hope. We can face our circumstances with an assurance that our God, our creator, and our source, intends for us to succeed and is always there to aid in our deliverance. Besides, somewhere else there is somebody depending on us to survive. Someone else, whether they be in the present or appear years from now, is dependent upon our example, our precedent, from which they can find the inspiration they need to overcome their specific obstacles. Each of our victorious testimonies will become a necessary record for those around us and after us, in order for them to be victorious as well. Someone else is dependent upon our prayers. There are individuals or groups of individuals, near and far, who need your specific prayer and support. So, there is much more riding on us, than our own lives. The welfare of many others is on the line; we simply cannot surrender hope.

CHAPTER 9: As I Go On.... (A Tribute to Allen Patterson)

Gregory Allen Patterson passed away on November 21, 2005. A host of family and friends bid him farewell – remembering the legacy he left behind.

Always a smile in his voice, Allen's politeness was genuine and his manner gentile. Upon meeting him, your eyes were quickly averted from the vehicle that seemed to envelop him to his handsome face. That's when it happens. Your eyes meet his, and for one brief moment you see the reflection of a soul that has found peace in what would be frustration for lesser men. His eyes spoke of calm waters where there could have been angry seas. Clear skies among gray clouds. They also display quiet determination that can only be found in a wilderness deep in the spirit: an unexplored strength that only God can bring forth. These eyes make your own heart start to believe on the impossible.

Just when you think that this individual could not make a more striking first impression, your eyes become fixated on his smile. There you find boldness and confidence: a grand stand statement about commitment, dedication and mercy. With kind eyes and a dazzling smile, he is no longer a stranger in a wheelchair, but rather, a familiar hero.

We all begin our journey in life the same way. Full of hope, vigor and wonder, but what distinguishes each of us is our degree of confidence. Allen was no exception. His journey began with ambition to discover new frontiers and to conquer them all. But too often our paths contain many difficult turns and obstacles. Some turns we maneuver with ease; others we struggle at the wheel. Some obstacles we just go around;

others we get out of the vehicle and remove. Allen's road contained all these difficulties as well. But what makes his travel so special is not the circumstances that detoured his journey, but the way Allen handled the vehicle. His journey was one of discovery. He discovered the essence of God, and who he was in God, and how both his spirit and the Spirit of God became one.

Allen learned that you can buckle up and plot the course, but there is no guarantee that you will reach the destination on time or as planned. Perhaps you may never reach the plotted destination at all. However, Allen understood that if you didn't, everything was still okay. Why? Because during the trip, if your mind and heart is open to God, you will receive knowledge and wisdom. You will receive guidance and assurance. And when you reach your destination, wherever it may be, you will be wiser and at peace. Allen certainly was.

As we read his story, we see that Allen's journey was filled with dangerous curves and unexpected bad weather. Sometimes the rain was so heavy that Allen could not see his way. But he realized that God guided him through. Sometimes the road washed out and Allen had to find another route or take a new path. These alternatives are often part of life's lessons, and with anguish and struggle Allen endured. Allen sometimes needed help on this new path, and often tried to find his way on his own. But he discovered that the path was much easier with the help from friends. Some of the friends were old; offering advice because they had traveled the same path. Some of the friends were new; offering directions to help him get back on the main road. Most importantly, Allen eventually opened himself to these people and to God. He thought he let God in, only to discover later that God was there all the time.

    My phone conversations with Allen were always refreshing. Although he had experienced bitterness, there were only sweet tones in his voice. Deep sadness and depression had once reigned in his life, but there was always laughter when we talked. Anger had dominated his attitude, but the sound of forgiveness echoed behind every word. Where frustration once stubbornly stood, contentment abounded with each statement he made. Allen discovered that he could be happy at the place he was until due time to move him further on his journey. Road rage never helped anyone or changed any situation, and Allen ascertained this fact and embraced it as he traveled his destined path. As he waited at each traffic jam, he soon found the path of least resistance to make his way through the slow-moving chaos. Allen emerged with wisdom; about himself and God.

    As Allen moved deeper into God, he realized that a relationship is exactly what God wanted. Allen loved and needed God, and he was not ashamed to tell this truth to the whole world. Relationships are hard work, and that is exactly what Allen did. He anxiously pursued his relationship with God, and found what was there all along: love. A love so strong that it shifted the focus of an angry young man from his own tragedy to the needs of others. A love that turned the frown of despair into a smile of optimism. There was nothing negative about the man I met. In his demeanor there were only rays of sunshine and rainbows, and I could not help but smile at the sound of his voice.

So the dashing, confident captain we met at the beginning returns to us at the end of the journey. He possesses the same qualities, but in a different way. He has been renewed by the hand of God and enabled by God's blessing. He has searched and reached deep inside to let his spirit man determine who he is and what his destiny would be. He has aligned the purpose of his life with God's will, and everyone who encountered him was the better for it. At least I was. As I reflect back, I wish I could have known him better. I remember his smile, and how I felt as though he knew something I did not, and whatever this great mystery was, it warmed his very soul. Reading his story, Allen revealed the hidden secret: the truth about God's love and our love for others; God dwelling in us and how we should dwell in God. And finally, knowing who we are in God and that all things are possible through Him. God is big enough for any situation or circumstance. Allen showed us the way.

Going Home
The shoreline's familiar shape comes into sight
As the lighthouse beacon cut the sky like spears,
Like rain from the floodgates of heaven
My eyes are open and filled with tears.
Tears that express joy and relief
Tears that resound my journey's end
Tears that speak of my personal victory
Tears of gratitude to my dearest Friend.
For God has revealed Himself to me
And revealed to me who I am
That I am depended on Him
And I have victory though the blood of the Lamb.
So this young captain is prepared to exit his ship
Because his destination has been found
And as he enters this land of heavenly bliss
He will cherish every smell, every sight and every sound.

~Glendora Little Moore

ISBN 142513753-9